The Merrill Ream 10-Lesson
Speed Reading Course

The Merrill Ream 10-Lesson
Speed Reading Course

Merrill L. Ream

Sheed Andrews and McMeel, Inc.
Subsidiary of Universal Press Syndicate
Kansas City

First Printing, July 1977
Second Printing, December 1977

Library of Congress Cataloging in Publication Data

Ream, Merrill L
    The Merrill Ream 10-lesson speed reading course.

    1. Rapid reading. I. Title. II. Title: 10-lesson
speed reading course.
LB1050.54.R4   428.4'3   77-24102
ISBN 0-8362-0752-1

Acknowledgments

To RMR, of course

Ten stories were commissioned for use in this book. One story appears in each of the ten lessons and they are used in the testing process. The authors are:

Harold Casey
George Class
Robert Coath
Jeanette Coyle
Gene Gregston
Robert Haven
Ralph Margolis
Merrill L. Ream
Terese M. Sutor

PREFACE

The author of this speed reading book is to be applauded for his work and the attempt to improve the ability of all citizens to more effectively cope with the explosion in the quantity and variety of the instruments of written communication. Both those readers who seriously desire to advance from a relatively low level of reading accomplishment and those who read more effectively should respond. Both will bring different problems to the effort which is basically a self-administered, self-disciplined, and self-motivated one.

Probably those readers with the most difficult task are the ones with a legacy of poor education in the earlier school years. Hopefully, the worst of the mediocre education, the procrastination or unwillingness to change, the ill-chosen and inappropriate materials for reading, is behind us. It needs to be behind us for failure at this point brings boredom and inattentiveness which infects the breadth of the school curriculum and the adult post-school life.

This bit of history is very important because for those in greatest need of reading improvement it is vital that the instruments of improvement clearly light the way to progress. The careful orchestration of the lessons, with measures of attainment enabling quick recognition of gains in reading progress, is basic. The selection of the reading rate and comprehension test stories is realistic and should be a very positive influence.

Self-discipline is required of the participant in the speed reading program and careful adherence to the lessons can be expected to have obvious and early rewards. Furthermore, this success is of great importance. To read inefficiently or not at all means for some the inability to progress onward or even hold desired jobs. It also means failure to sufficiently understand the world around us because of inadequate reading accomplishments.

One may hope that such efforts, as just mentioned, will also bring an overall educational gain within the schools across the broad spectrum of students. The "remedial" courses at the college level bespeak a waste of resources and potential both in the earlier school years and at the college level; wastes which the individuals and the nation can ill afford. Experience at the university level, from the freshman class into the graduate sector, brings continuing evidence of this unfortunate situation.

Success is greatly to be desired in school and later life. I wish this speed reading program the best.

Dr. J.O. McClintic
— Professor Emeritus
— San Diego State University

TABLE OF CONTENTS

Lesson One
YOUR PRESENT READING RATE AND COMPREHENSION

I completed seven years of college and still wasn't aware of a need to gain speed reading skills. I plodded through countless books, magazines, pamphlets, and what have you at a slow reading rate. It took the parent of a former student of mine to point out that a great deal is done for students in school who have reading deficiencies. He looked at a well-equipped reading laboratory and mentioned that his son, then attending Stanford University, was faced with reading an amount of material that was overwhelming. This parent wanted to know why something couldn't be done for the student who was a capable reader but didn't know how to read fast. This made sense to me. I did some research on speed reading (sometime before it became fashionable), enlisted the aid of some motivated students, and through a process of trial and error we all learned to read fast. This book is a result of these early beginnings and over ten years of refinement in aiding thousands of students to read fast with comprehension.

The material in this book will be presented in lessons which comprise a total speed reading course. Each chapter will follow a basic format which includes: 1) Opening Statement, 2) Skills and Techniques, 3) Goal Setting, 4) Rate and Comprehension Test, and 5) Practice Before the Next Lesson.

OPENING STATEMENT

I suggest that you spend at least one week on the activities in each lesson in order to assist you in the mastery of the speed reading techniques and skills necessary to move on to subsequent lessons. Essentially, the reading material in this book presents a "Bare Bones" approach to speed reading in that you will learn about techniques of speed reading but you will have to implement them in your reading style all by yourself. You will identify poor reading habits, establish good reading habits, and master the techniques of speed reading. There is no magic formula to develop speed reading. You must learn good reading techniques, practice, and then read faster with satisfactory comprehension.

What is reading? Simply, reading consists of recognizing words (vocabulary) and understanding what you read (comprehension). Everything that you do in the speed reading course presented in this book will enhance your ability to develop vocabulary and comprehension skills while reading at a faster rate.

The following statistical charts will show the reader the reading rate and comprehension achievement scores of some reading students who participated in a speed reading program on a secondary school level. The students operated in a reading laboratory, had daily instruction and practice, and had a teacher available to answer their questions. These circumstances have to be the best of conditions under which to become proficient in speed reading. These students used some reading machines to aid in mastery of skills and techniques, but they also used the basic speed reading course that is presented in this book.

The students attended class for 50 minutes a day,

five days a week, for seven weeks. The reading rate averages are compiled from the test scores of over 100 students involved in the program using weekly reading rate and comprehension scores. The level of difficulty of the testing material is commensurate with the age group of the students.

Reading Rate Chart

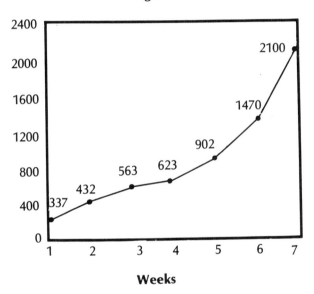

Weeks

Analysis of the reading rate chart shows that the average words per minute (WPM) read progresses in a slow but steady manner until the final two weeks when a dramatic spurt in WPM takes place. Statistical charting of rate and comprehension scores of college age and adult speed reading students show a similar rate pattern developing in the final weeks of their course. The slow growth in the early weeks can be attributed to getting rid of poor reading habits. As mastery of the speed reading skills necessary to read fast takes place, reading rates steadily increase. The large increase in reading rate (WPM) in the final several weeks can be attributed to students having mastered speed reading skills, a willingness to read faster, and increasing self-confidence in the application of their new speed reading abilities.

After students are statistically shown that people can read much faster, the students' usual reaction is "Aha! They won't understand what they have read!" The following statistical chart on comprehension involves the same students as in the previous rate chart. A comprehension test was administered each week immediately following the rate test. Average comprehension scores are expressed in percentages.

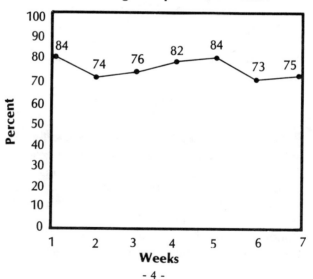

Reading Comprehension Chart

Analysis of the comprehension chart shows that when you compare the weekly comprehension and reading rate chart scores, you can read much faster and with satisfactory comprehension.

The following information is presented to acquaint the reader with the intelligence levels necessary to read fast and with comprehension. An experiment was conducted, using the same materials and speed reading techniques that were used by students whose rate and comprehension scores were presented in the preceding charts, in which eight identified gifted students (148 I.Q. or above) and eight control group volunteer students, all on the secondary school level, attended class for 25 minutes daily, five days a week, for a nine week period. The following charts present the reading rate and comprehension results.

Reading Rate Chart

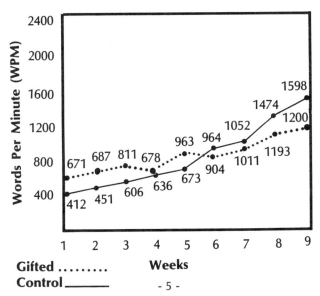

Gifted .... **Weeks**
Control _____

Analysis of the reading rate chart shows that the gifted students read faster initially than the control group volunteer students. A reading rate progression occurs as both student groups mastered the speed reading techniques at the end of the experiment. Both groups achieved somewhat similar reading rate results.

The next chart shows the comprehension scores of the gifted and control volunteer students. Average comprehension scores are expressed in percentages.

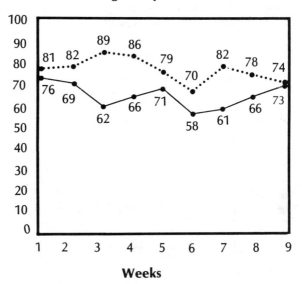

Reading Comprehension Chart

Weeks

Gifted ·······
Control _____

Analysis of the comprehension chart shows that the gifted students comprehended at a higher level initially than the control group volunteer students. As the course progressed both groups followed a somewhat similar comprehension pattern until both groups reached a common level at the end of the nine weeks.

To sum up the results of the preceding four charts, the reader can ascertain that high reading rates can be achieved while still maintaining satisfactory comprehension. Also, it isn't necessary to have a brilliant mind in order to read fast with comprehension. Reading rate and comprehension scores achieved by college and adult level speed reading students in other experiments show somewhat similar patterns.

In this lesson you are going to find out how fast you read and how well you comprehend what you read. You will read a story later on in this lesson and be tested over its contents. A Reading Rate Record Graph and Reading Comprehension Record Graph that you will use is included on pages 177-178 at the end of this book. Record reading rate and comprehension test results on these charts for each lesson so that you can see your reading progress in the weeks to come.

SKILLS AND TECHNIQUES

In this first lesson you are going to find out the "awful truth!" In other words, how fast you read and how well you comprehend what you read. For each of the ten lessons in this book, you will take a Rate and Comprehension Test. Each lesson contains a story that you will read. You will need to keep track of the time it takes you to read the test story and answer questions about the story. You will mark down the time it takes you to read the story in minutes and seconds. The test stories were selected for readability and have a level of difficulty gauged to be of an average or normal level. Following each story are ten comprehension questions which you will start to answer immediately after you finish reading the story.

While taking this initial Rate and Comprehension Test I suggest that you use your normal reading manner. This will tell you how fast you have been reading and how well you understand what you have been reading. Take a reasonable amount of time to answer the comprehension questions. You shouldn't look back into the story for answers to questions.

It is very important to keep accurate reading rate and comprehension records for purposes of comparison and goal setting. After each story is a reading rate chart that you will use to convert your reading time to your reading rate which is expressed in words per minute (WPM). Turn to page 177 . You will find a Reading Rate Record Graph. Find the column for test #1 and write the exact WPM above it. Darken the column up to the WPM you achieve. Reading rate figures are shown on the left margin. Place the date you took the test at the top of the column. Follow these same steps for each lesson to chart your reading rate progress.

Turn to page 178 . You will find a Reading Comprehension Record Graph. After you have checked your answers against the answer key at the end of this lesson, find test #1, darken the column up to the correct number of answers you achieve, and place the date you took the test at the top of the column. Follow these same steps for each lesson to chart your comprehension progress.

In subsequent Rate and Comprehension Tests you will put to use the kinds of speed reading and comprehension skills that you learn about in each lesson.

GOAL SETTING

At this point your goal is to commit yourself to do the ten lessons in this book that are necessary to read faster and with comprehension. This will require that you have the discipline to spend an adequate amount of time to practice and master the skills and techniques of speed reading in this book. It is always very important to maintain a positive attitude toward your lessons. You must be willing to experiment with old, and probably bad, reading patterns in an effort to establish good reading practices. Choose a place in your home or place of employment where you will always, if possible, go to do your lessons from now on.

It is also your goal to find out how fast you have been reading all these years and what your comprehension level is. It is suggested that you read the test story presented in this lesson in your regular reading manner. Knowing your reading rate and comprehension level will not only be interesting for you to know, but it will also establish the base from which you will grow in reading rate and comprehension.

RATE AND COMPREHENSION TEST

Read the following story, "Moray." Be sure to refer to the procedure for taking this test that was described under the Skills and Techniques section of this lesson. *Do the following for each of the ten Rate and Comprehension Tests in this book:*

1)   Read the story,

2) Keep track of the time taken to read the story in minutes and seconds and *write it down,*

3) Take the comprehension test,

4) Use the chart at the end of the lesson to figure your reading rate (WPM),

5) Use the answer key at the end of the lesson to figure your comprehension level,

6) Chart your scores on the Reading Rate and Comprehension graphs on pages 177 and 178 ,

7) You will need a watch, or some type of timepiece, on which to keep track of the time it takes you to read the test story,

8) Think of your goal which in this lesson is to read the story in your normal reading manner.

* * Set your timepiece — read the story * *

MORAY

by Harold D. Casey

Kevin Green and his youngest brother, Mark, dropped the anchor of their small aluminum skiff near the west tip of Anacapa Island, a small barren island eleven miles offshore from the city of Oxnard, California. They watched the anchor, with attached manila line, descend through the clear blue waters of the Pacific Ocean to a sandy, boulder-littered bottom some fifty or sixty feet below the surface.

They were anchored only ten or fifteen yards from the island, in an area called the "Fish Bowl" by

Scuba divers, where the island's cliffs rise almost vertically to a height of about 930 feet above sea level. Below sea level the cliffs have crevices harboring flower-like green anemones, purple and red spiny urchins, bright red shrub-like gorgonians, pink and green abalone, ruby lipped scallops, lobsters, and moray eels. The boulders at the base of the cliff provide attachment for kelp holdfasts and the dense brown kelp forest, swaying in endless rhythm to the ocean tides and currents, provide food and refuge for countless numbers and varieties of fish.

After strapping on their weight belts and scuba tanks, filled with compressed air, both Kevin and Mark slipped over the side of the skiff and followed the anchor rope to the ocean bottom. Kevin, carrying an abalone iron in his right hand and a "goodie" bag in his left, was intent on harvesting abalones and lobsters for their evening meal. Mark carried an underwater spear gun with the intention of spearing a black sea bass.

As the two divers swam among the tangled kelp fronds, Mark observed a pair of yellow rimmed eyes and the blunt mottled brown snout of an animal extending from a rocky crevice. A more experienced diver would have immediately recognized the creature as a moray eel and would have avoided it. Mark, however, released the safety catch of his spear gun, aimed, and pulled the trigger. The three rubber bands, attached to the spear gun, drove a stainless steel barbed shaft completely through the center of the moray's head. Mark, assuming that the eel was dead, dived down to retrieve his game. When he grabbed the shaft of the spear and tugged on it, the eel raised its head high and struck viciously at the diver's face.

When Mark instinctively raised his arm for protection, the eel grasped his entire arm in its jaws and its knife-like teeth inflicted terrible wounds.

The eel let loose at once and both divers made their way to the surface. Kevin laboriously pulled his injured brother into the skiff, applied a tourniquet to stop the hemorrhage, started the outboard motor, and headed for the mainland. Fortunately, Mark survived the vicious attack and recovered the use of his arm but only after being hospitalized for three months. Mark Green, like so many fishermen and divers in all tropical and south temperate seas, had had his first encounter with the notoriously aggressive and vicious moray eel.

More than 120 species of morays have been described and vary in size from about three to ten feet in length. Only minute anatomical variations distinguish the many confusing species. Members of the genus *Gymnothorax*, referring to the fact that morays lack both pelvic and pectoral fins, are the most common, largest, and probably the most dangerous of the morays.

Morays rarely attack without provocation but are capable of inflicting serious wounds on their enemies, including man. Their bite is considered to be poisonous by some authorities although there are conflicting opinions on their venomous qualities.

The larval form of the moray eel is quite unlike a full grown parent and assume a transparent, leaf-like form. The discovery of their life history reads much like a detective story and indeed much of the story remains untold. Early naturalists advanced most extraordinary and unscientific theories as to the manner in which eels reproduce. The ancient Greeks attributed Jupiter as the procreator of eels as were all children whose paternity was doubtful. Over 2000 years ago, Aristotle pointed out that eels seemed to possess no reproductive organs and therefore must be derived out of the "bowels of the earth" presumably by some means of spontaneous generation. This view was also held by the poet-fisherman Isaak Walton. Pliny suggested that eels had no sex and believed that they rubbed themselves against rocks and that the pieces scraped off came to life. During the Middle Ages, the birth of eels was attributed to the dews of May mornings or they were said to come from the gills or other fish. One extraordinary theory, advanced by a Mr. Cairncross in 1862, was that a beetle was the progenitor of eels.

The first marine larval eel was discovered in 1763 by William Morris but was not described until 1788 when the naturalist Gmelin named it after its finder. In 1861 Carus recognized that this creature was a larval form rather than an adult fish and in 1864 it was established that it was the larval stage of a conger eel. Three Italian investigators, Raffaele, Grasse, and Colundruccio, were able to trace the transformation of several kinds of larvae into their respective adult species. Finally in 1936, the reproductive mystery was solved when the development of the egg of an unknown species of deep-sea eel was photographed as the hatching took place. This event was vividly described by William Beebe.

Recent observations of the life history of a marine eel showed that the female deposited her eggs far below the surface. The male eel fertilized the eggs while they floated in the cold darkness of the water. One naturalist observed the breeding habits of the male eel and noted that he gripped the swimming female in his jaws for hours before fertilization of the eggs took place. The eggs are large, compared with most fish, and measure about one-eighth of an inch in diameter. They are so transparent that only the yolk and periphery is visible. The eggs rise slowly toward the surface and pass through the earliest stages that are common to all animal life which is still mysterious and inexplicable.

Soon after fertilization, a thickened saucer-like mass of protoplasm at one end of the cell slowly divides into equal cells. Cell division continues by 4, 8, 16, 32, 64, and so on until a finely divided froth of thousands of cells completely encircles the yolk. Within the next hundred hours or so, a perfect little eel develops. Its heart beats steadily and the unseeing eyes move in their sockets. Its parrot-like jaws open and close, the neck muscles move, and the sharp beak continues to rub against the inner lining of its transparent shell.

In time the jaws break through, the head follows, then with one or two convulsive jerks the eel is born. The entire time, from fertilization to hatching, requires about a week. A short time after emerging, the larva measures almost half an inch from head to tail and is as flat and transparent as a piece of cellophane. Within a day the eel learns to orient its body, keep right side up, to swim straight ahead, and dart from side to side. The tissues about its parrot-like beak shrivel and its needle-like teeth are bared to their roots. A parrot is transformed into a sabre-toothed tiger in the plankton world!

Certain species of eel larvae attain a length of a foot or more and one three-foot specimen has been captured. Even more astonishing is that once the larvae have achieved their maximum size, the eel grows by shrinking! After several stages of progressive shrinking, the flat, transparent larval eel changes into the serpentine form of the adult. As the juveniles grow into adults they add vertebrae to their backbone. This is also true of the adult eels in that they continue to add vertebrae as they increase in body length. It is fortunate that these creatures do not grow 60 feet or more as they would put to shame every effort of man's imagination to create dragons or sea serpents.

* * * * * * * * * *

IMMEDIATELY START TO ANSWER THE FOLLOWING TEN COMPREHENSION QUESTIONS. CIRCLE THE *MOST* CORRECT ANSWER. TAKE A REASONABLE AMOUNT OF TIME TO ANSWER THE QUESTIONS. YOU SHOULDN'T LOOK BACK INTO THE STORY FOR ANSWERS.

* * * * * * * * * *

COMPREHENSION TEST ONE

___ 1) About how many species of moray eels are there? a) 6, b) 120, c) 1050.

___ 2) Early naturalists advanced many theories as to how eels reproduce that border on a) superstition, b) scientific fact, c) observation.

___ 3) Compared with other fish the eggs of an eel are a) microscopic, b) quite large, c) deposited on the surface of the water.

___ 4) The parrot-like beak of the larval eel is used a) to hatch from the egg, b) to gather food, c) to protect itself from enemies.

___ 5) Once the larval eel reaches its maximum size it grows a) through cell division, b) to a length of 60 feet, c) by shrinking.

___ 6) Which of the following is not true of the moray eel? a) aggressive, b) serpentine, c) non-vertebrate.

___ 7) Although it isn't stated in the story, probably an effective defense the moray eel has is a) hiding in rock crevices, b) swimming ability, c) a fearsome appearance.

___ 8) The author suggests that a diver's best defense against a moray eel is a) the spear gun, b) to leave the eel alone, c) to be accompanied by a fellow diver.

___ 9) In which of the following seas is the moray eel most unlikely to be found? a) tropical, b) south temperate, c) high latitude.

___ 10) Mainly this story is about a) an encounter with a moray eel, b) the physical development of the moray eel, c) misconceptions about the moray eel.

* * * * * * * * * *

CHECK YOUR ANSWERS AGAINST THE KEY ON PAGE 17. CONVERT YOUR READING TIME TO RATE USING THE CHART ON PAGE 18. BY THE WAY, ONCE YOU HAVE CONVERTED READING TIME INTO WORDS PER MINUTE (WPM) IT IS NO LONGER NECESSARY TO KEEP A RECORD OF THE READING TIME THAT IT TAKES YOU TO READ EACH STORY. CHART YOUR READING RATE (WPM) AND COMPREHENSION SCORE ON THE READING RATE GRAPH AND READING COMPREHENSION GRAPH ON PAGES 177 AND 178.

* * * * * * * * * *

PRACTICE BEFORE THE NEXT LESSON

Commit yourself to doing the ten speed reading lessons in this book. Make a list of the kinds of materials that you like to read. Keep these materials in the place you have chosen to do your lessons so that you can use them for practicing your speed reading techniques. Use all the materials in this book with the knowledge that mastering them will allow you to read faster with satisfactory comprehension.

At this point, you might check your first reading rate and comprehension scores against the rates achieved by those students that were shown on the charts earlier in this lesson. Before you move onto Lesson Two, plan to spend at least several hours, over a period of several days, on the following two activities: 1) Read some simple materials such as are presented in newspaper-like columns. 2) Force yourself to read faster and read down the column of printed materials. Be very aware that you are trying to read faster!

Students in my regular school classes have achieved very high reading rates. Some read several thousand words per minute with satisfactory comprehension! All students certainly don't read this fast, but you can use these proven speed reading methods to develop improved speed with satisfactory comprehension.

* * * * * * * * *

Answers — Comprehension Test One — 1) b, 2) a, 3) b, 4) a, 5) c, 6) c, 7) a, 8) b, 9) c, 10) b

* * * * * * * * *

Time	Rate—WPM	Time	Rate—WPM
1:00	1329	5:00	266
1:10	1139	5:10	257
1:20	997	5:20	249
1:30	886	5:30	242
1:40	797	5:40	235
1:50	725	5:50	228
2:00	665	6:00	221
2:10	613	6:10	216
2:20	570	6:20	210
2:30	532	6:30	204
2:40	498	6:40	199
2:50	469	6:50	194
3:00	443	7:00	190
3:10	420	7:10	183
3:20	399	7:20	181
3:30	380	7:30	177
3:40	362	7:40	173
3:50	347	7:50	170
4:00	332	8:00	166
4:10	319	8:10	163
4:20	307	8:20	159
4:30	295	8:30	156
4:40	285	8:40	153
4:50	275	8:50	150

Lesson Two
HOW YOU READ

What kinds of people become speed reading students? Students that I have known range in age from ten to over seventy years of age and have backgrounds as varied as psychiatrists, nuns, policemen, ministers, authors, engineers, sportscasters, newspaper reporters, publishers, teachers, housewives, students of all ages, and so on.

What results can you expect from mastering the speed reading techniques presented in this book? The aforementioned types of students have developed reading rates over 2000 words per minute (WPM) with satisfactory comprehension. Everyone doesn't read this fast, but it is possible to read faster by using good speed reading techniques. Students have attested to the reading rates that were presented in the charts in Lesson One through letters, testimonials, and statistical evidence. Thousands of students that I have taught have achieved some measure of reading success using the same techniques of speed reading that you are going to learn and use. You can expect to double your present reading rate; many of you will do even better, and still have satisfactory comprehension with the proper effort on your part.

OPENING STATEMENT

I feel that the best aid to increased comprehension and a faster reading rate is to *preview* materials you are going to read. Book reviews that appear on book covers or jackets provide a guide to the contents of the story and essentially constitute a preview. Here is a plan to set up a story for previewing: 1) Read the title; 2) Read the first paragraph or two and the last paragraph; 3) Read sub-titles and chapter titles; and 4) Study pictures, charts, etc. Do these things before you begin to read the entire story.

Stories may not contain all the above but the method is psychologically sound. To illustrate the psychological learning aspects involved, look at a house or building near you. Your first impression is of seeing the house or building in its total configuration. This is analogous to previewing a story and gaining an overall view of what you are going to read. Now back to the house or building. Continue to look and you begin to see windows, doors, plants, colors, design, or in other words, the parts that make up the house or building. This is analogous to reading the words and parts making up the story after having done a preview. The learning pattern involved is known as Gestalt or field psychology.

The prior knowledge of what you are going to read gained by previewing and then actually reading all parts of the story will enable you to read with greater speed and comprehension. Previewing is like studying a road map of the route you are going to follow while on vacation. It isn't necessary to preview all materials you read but if comprehension is an absolute necessity, as it often is for people such as students, preview.

Radio and television newscasters warm-up their reading voice before going on the air by reading aloud. You too need to use a warm-up before you read your test story. However, you should always read silently when warming-up. Before previewing or reading your test story, "lubricate" your reading style by selecting a story *over which you have already been tested!* For several minutes read the story practicing those speed reading techniques you are now learning. The reason for choosing a story you have already read is that the familiarity with the contents of the story will relieve your comprehension worries and allow you to concentrate on the skills necessary to read fast. Remember to warm-up before reading any of the remaining test stories in this book.

SKILLS AND TECHNIQUES

As a speed reader it is important that you understand what your eyes do while reading and the importance of basic eye movements. Let us start with how your eyes *don't* move while reading. Panning is moving your eyes in a continuous motion without stopping to see any one thing in particular. Photographers use panning techniques with both still and motion pictures. Since the eye and the lens of a camera are similar, the following illustration will demonstrate panning. We have all been observers of home movies of the amateur photographer. For instance, he steps fearlessly to the edge of the Grand Canyon with his motion picture camera and pans from left to right, usually too quickly, in a 180 degree arc. The results are often blurred when shown to his polite but suffering guests because even motion picture cameras can't cope with too quick a panning movement. The same is true of the human eye.

The reason for this long discussion on panning, which is how you don't read, is to save you some time while learning speed reading. I have found many students attempting to pan across pages of

printed material moving their heads. Some students even move their books across before their eyes while keeping their head stationary. Let's get on to what your eyes must do to read.

The first basic eye movement is called an eye *fix*. When you read, your eyes do not flow smoothly across the written words but instead fix (stop), jerk to other words, fix again, jerk, fix, and on and on. Your eye *must* fix (stop) to read. Have another person read a book and you look over the top of the book and observe the eye fixes which are readily noticeable.

Another eye movement is the *return sweep*. This is when your eyes have reached the right hand portion of the printed line of words and in a sweeping motion move back to the left to pick up the next lower line of words. View this eye movement by having a person read a book in the same manner as when you observed eye fixes. Students have often remarked that the return sweep appears like a typewriter carriage being returned to the left.

To help you understand the basic eye movements of eye fixes and the return sweep, the following is a graphic representation of both. Imagine the horizontal lines to be words, the X's as eye fixes, and the diagonal line moving from the right back to the left to the lower line of words as the return sweep:

Now, what is the significance of eye fixes and the return sweep for speed reading? Suppose you could, through practice of good speed reading techniques, reduce the number of eye fixes necessary to read words to the two inside fixes, getting rid of the far left and right eye fixes, and shortening the return sweep to between the two inside eye fixes. Following is a graphic representation of this:

Essentially you have doubled your reading rate! You will practice speed reading techniques to help you reduce the number of eye fixes and shorten the return sweep in future lessons.

GOAL SETTING

1) You will need to view the basic eye movements of eye fixes and the return sweep and understand their significance in the speed reading process. 2) Before you get ready to read the test story, warm-up by reading, for several minutes, a story that you have already read, preferably from this book. You could warm-up on the test story from Lesson One. From now on, warm-up in this fashion before reading any of the remaining test stories in this book. Force yourself to read fast! 3) Previewing - Make it your goal to master this most important reading skill. It will enable you to read with greater comprehension and with increased speed. Remember to preview the test story in Lesson Two by a) reading the title, b) reading the first paragraph, c) glancing through the entire story, and then d) reading the last paragraph.

Allow yourself *thirty seconds* to preview the test story. *Do not* count this time against the time it will take you to read the test story. After you have previewed the entire story, go back to the beginning and start reading for time. I cannot overemphasize the importance of the preview as a speed reading skill!

* * * * * * * * * *

RATE AND COMPREHENSION TEST

Read the following story, "A Visit to Mt. Vernon." Be sure to refer to the procedure for taking this test that was described under the Skills and Techniques section of Lesson One. Do this right now. *Do the following for this and each of the ten Rate and Comprehension Tests in this book:*

1) Read the story,

2) Keep track of the time taken to read the story in minutes and seconds and *write it down,*

3) Take the comprehension test,

4) Use the chart at the end of the lesson to figure your reading rate (WPM),

5) Use the answer key at the end of the lesson to figure your comprehension level,

6) Chart your scores on the Reading Rate and Comprehension Graphs on pages 177 and 178.

7) You will need a watch, or some type of timepiece, on which to keep track of the time it takes to read the test story,

8) Think of your goal, which in this lesson is to preview the test story in the manner described in the Goal Setting portion of this lesson.

* * * * * * * * * *

* * Set your timepiece — read the story * *

A VISIT TO MT. VERNON

by Merrill L. Ream

George Washington, the father of our country; namesake of Washington, D.C.; the Washington Monument; and his likeness on the most commonly used currency, the dollar bill. Who can forget the cherry tree incident or seeing his picture displayed in public buildings. Washington, in Masonic trappings, laid the cornerstone of the United States Capitol building. In the Smithsonian Institution in Washington, D.C., is displayed the tent and bed used by George Washington while serving as Commander of the Revolutionary War Army.

The years of vicarious exposure to this grand personage had honed my anticipation to what had been a lifelong desire. At last I was to visit Washington's home, Mt. Vernon, and see vistas his eyes had known and share the ground where his feet had trod.

From Washington, D.C., my wife and I started the drive to Mt. Vernon, the home of George Washington, on a lovely August morning. Flanked by the Potomac River, sparkling in the sunlight, and the lush green foliage of the Virginia countryside, dotted with stately homes, our drive continued along the same route that George Washington must have traveled many times himself.

George Washington's brother Lawrence named the estate in honor of Admiral Vernon and George purchased it from his deceased brother's wife and eventually enlarged the land area to 8000 acres. The mansion, in Washington's words, was "pleasantly situated" on a commanding eminence overlooking the Potomac and low Maryland hills to the east. The estate is one of the best remaining examples of an eighteenth century southern plantation. Mt. Vernon is owned and maintained by the Mt. Vernon Ladies' Association of the Union. This group purchased the estate from the Washington family in 1853, using money raised through public subscription, and is dedicated to the preservation of the home and tomb of General Washington.

Members of the Ladies' Association conduct tours of the mansion and grounds. We entered the home directly into the large Banquet Hall which was built by George Washington to accommodate the many visitors to his home. Hepplewhite sideboards, paintings, and gifts from admirers adorn this impressive room. We passed into the central hall which extends the full width of the mansion and allows views into other ground floor rooms.

Steps lead to the second floor and the Lafayette bedroom so called after its distinguished occupant. There are four additional bedrooms on the second floor including the bedchamber of General and Martha Washington. A lady visitor in front of us remarked about the "delightful" musty odor of the room. A third floor of the house contains bedrooms and storerooms but isn't opened during the busy summer season.

Coming downstairs, we paused in General Washington's library and moved into a hallway which allowed views into a first floor bedroom and the family dining room. This area is located directly under the second floor bedrooms and dressing areas used by members of the Washington family. I remarked to a Ladies' Association guide of a perfume-like odor that pervaded the area. She stated that the odor was like that of powder used on wigs worn by both men and women of Washington's time. She said that the odor was always present in that part of the house and suggested that excess amounts of the powder were trapped in the cracks of the plank flooring above. Yet powdered wigs went out of style over 150 years ago!

As we prepared to look at other parts of the estate outside the mansion, our friendly Ladies' Association guide invited us to return for a second tour of the house and sniff the odors present in the various rooms. We then passed the pantry with its china, glassware, wines, and cordials and finally a small room, which would now be termed a "mudroom," containing a coat, boots, and a walking stick belonging to George Washington.

We toured the grounds and outbuildings of the estate including the tomb of George and Martha and other members of the Washington family. Then, as the wine taster clears his palate with bread, my wife and I cleared our olfactory senses with the clean Virginia air and began to retrace our steps through the mansion, sniffing as we went. No special odors were noticed in the Banquet Hall, but just off this room was the Little Parlor with its paintings and the harpsichord used by the women of the Washington family This room contained a distinct musty odor that we hadn't noticed before! Upstairs we again noticed the heavy musty smell in General and Martha Washington's bedroom. Downstairs we discussed odors with our Ladies' Association guide who had in our absence sniffed the pantry area and noticed a cornmeal-like smell. We sniffed. Was it the power of suggestion? There seemed to be a cornmeal-like odor! Yet, according to our guide, no genteel Virginia planter would be eating a "Yankee" concoction made from cornmeal. Could all those years George Washington spent in northern states have sharpened his appetite for cornmeal dishes which were surreptitiously enjoyed in the pantry and whose odor still remained! We wondered how a house built over 200 years ago and last lived in over 100 years ago still retained "Yankee" cornmeal and musty odors along with the smell of wig powder.

I just had to ask our informative Ladies' Association guide if there were ghosts at Mt. Vernon. She hesitated, said her husband felt she shouldn't talk about such things, but that the night guards believed that there were ghosts in the mansion! The house is protected by two electronic alarm systems. At night the guards sometimes hear heavy footsteps in the house and surmise that someone is in the mansion and that the dual alarm systems are inoperative. The guards then rush into the house to apprehend the offenders and immediately the alarms are set off proving that the system is in working order!

There were many intriguing incidents associated with our visit. The beauty and history of Mt. Vernon was fascinating, but the other "extras" were really frosting on the cake.

* * * * * * * * *

COMPREHENSION TEST TWO

___ 1) Mt. Vernon is located in a) Maryland b) District of Columbia, c) Virginia.

____ 2) Although it isn't mentioned in the story, George Washington was a) the father of our country, b) President of the United States, c) Commander of the Revolutionary Army.

____ 3) The visit to Mt. Vernon occurred during the a) spring, b) summer, c) fall.

____ 4) Most visitors to Mr. Vernon probably use which sense the most while touring the estate? a) smell b) sight c) touch.

____ 5) A reason that the guide at Mr. Vernon hesitated to discuss the possibility of ghosts could be that a) she wanted to write a book on the subject, b) she was afraid of losing her job, c) such supernatural things detract from the image projected about George Washington.

____ 6) Mt. Vernon was last lived in about how many years ago? a) 100, b) 50, c) 150.

____ 7) The room at Mt. Vernon that contained the perfume-like odor was the a) bedroom, b) dining room, c) library.

____ 8) The most logical explanation for the musty odor in the bedchamber of George and Martha Washington would be a) ghosts are associated with such an odor, b) the bedding and clothing there, c) the only entry is by one door.

____ 9) It is implied that cornmeal dishes were mainly enjoyed by a) inhabitants from southern states, b) soldiers in the Continental Army, c) inhabitants from northern states.

____ 10) Mainly this story is about a) some unexpected things found at Mt. Vernon, b) the buildings, grounds, and furnishings at Mt. Vernon, c) a tribute to George Washington.

* * * * * * * * * *

CHECK YOUR ANSWERS AGAINST THE KEY ON PAGE 31. CONVERT YOUR READING TIME TO RATE USING THE CHART ON PAGE 31. REMEMBER, ONCE YOU H AVE CONVERTED READING TIME INTO WORDS PER MINUTE (WPM) IT IS NO LONGER NECESSARY TO KEEP A RECORD OF THE READING TIME THAT IT TAKES YOU TO READ EACH STORY. CHART YOUR READING RATE (WPM) AND COMPREHENSION SCORE ON THE READING RATE GRAPH AND READING COMPREHENSION GRAPH ON PAGES 177 AND 178.

* * * * * * * * * *

PRACTICE BEFORE THE NEXT LESSON

How does your reading rate on Lesson Two compare with your rate on Lesson One? You should spend several hours on the following items before attempting Lesson Three.

1) Set your mind to "think" speed reading while practicing on the speed reading techniques presented in Lesson Two.

2) Remember the importance of a warm-up before reading any of the test stories.

3) Practice the skill of previewing. Choose some newspaper or magazine articles, or the chapter of a book, and preview them in the manner prescribed earlier in this lesson. Make this most important speed reading skill an integral part of your reading style.

4) With a friend, identify eye fixes and the return sweep. At this point practice should consist of being aware of the two eye movements and a need to reduce the number and length of both.

5) Read simple, columnar materials as you practice the speed reading techniques presented in Lesson Two. Newspapers and magazines are good sources of columnar materials on which to practice.

* * * * * * * * * *

Answers — Comprehension Test Two — 1) c, 2) b, 3) b, 4) b, 5) c, 6) a, 7) c, 8) b, 9) c, 10) a.

* * * * * * * * * *

Time	Rate— WPM	Time	Rate— WPM
1:00	1008	4:00	252
1:10	864	4:10	242
1:20	756	4:20	233
1:30	672	4:30	224
1:40	605	4:40	216
1:50	550	4:50	209
2:00	504	5:00	202
2:10	465	5:10	195
2:20	432	5:20	189
2:30	403	5:30	183
2:40	378	5:40	178
2:50	356	5:50	173
3:00	336	6:00	168
3:10	318	6:10	163
3:20	302	6L20	159
3:30	288	6:30	155
3:40	275	6:40	151
3:50	263	6:50	148

Lesson Three
WHY YOU READ SLOWLY

Try to understand as completely as possible every aspect of speed reading. Such diverse items as eye movements, reading columnar materials, having a place where you regularly do your lessons, how to take rate and comprehension tests, etc., all are a part of learning speed reading and will provide an overall view of what is taking place as you practice and master the bits and pieces of those skills and techniques that make up speed reading. Mastery of these skills and techniques by you will eventually evolve into your total speed reading style.

The best of all situations in which to develop sound speed reading skills most effectively is in a reading laboratory environment. Here the student can utilize a variety of speed reading materials, reading machines, be motivated by the interaction with fellow students, and ask the teacher to clarify problems. However, in your case it is all up to you to follow directions and do lessons. You must motivate yourself and do the reading activities on your own. You can't ask questions or see demonstrations. So, in this less-than-adequate situation, try to keep a positive attitude toward your work.

OPENING STATEMENT

To learn to read fast with comprehension you will need to: 1) Use a variety of speed reading techniques, 2) Progress from the reading level you now possess, 3) Realize that progress takes place only after a period of time, 4) Maintain an experimental attitude toward your work, and

5) be able to overcome rationalizations such as a) "If I read fast I won't understand," This is not true and was statistically proven by the results shown in the charts in Lesson One. b) "I'm uncomfortable reading fast." You are uncomfortable because you are experimenting with old, poor, established reading habits, c) "It's not working," Give yourself and the techniques you are learning a chance to work by using them over a period of time.

Students sometimes feel that the key to speed reading is to learn certain secrets or that the ability to read fast will suddenly be attained. Others have felt that speed reading is an intellectual exercise that exists on a higher level that only the more intelligent might understand and master. This simply is not true. Learning to speed read is hard work. Speed reading is a very mechanical process in that you identify and rid yourself of poor reading habits; establish good ones; and practice a great deal. As you can ascertain, this is hardly an intellectual process.

SKILLS AND TECHNIQUES

Our present concern is the identification of poor reading habits and what you can do to overcome them. You will need to devote considerable time to this section of Lesson Three in order to recognize and correct poor reading habits because they are mainly what is short circuiting your power to read faster.

1) Finger tracing — Most of us have been victimized by the practical joker who, in a crowd of people, is pointing and looking up into the sky at some imaginary object. When a number of people are trying to locate the thing at which he is

pointing, he stops and laughs at our gullibility. People still fall for this old ruse because we are so conditioned to looking at where someone is pointing. Finger tracing is when you trace with your finger below the line of words and across the page. Because we are so used to looking at what the finger is pointing out, our eyes see that word at which the finger is pointed and little else. Your eyes can't see the phrases of words necessary to learning to read fast unless you get your finger out of there! If you must use a finger to read, place it in the margin or center of the page and move *downward,* but not across. Do you finger trace when you read?

2) Moving your head — Move only your eyes when you read. Reduce the number of eye fixes it takes you to read a line of words and there won't be head movement. By practicing your reading on columnar materials you won't be so inclined to move your head while reading. Have someone observe to see if you move your head when you read. If you do move your head, simply stop. Do you move your head when you read?

3) Regressions — Do you remember when you were in school and the teacher called upon a student to read orally from a book? There was always that one person who stumbled over the words, repeated himself, lost his place in the book, and re-read phrases of words. This practice is known as regression. In Lesson Two you observed the eye movements of eye fixes and the return sweep. Maybe you also noticed the eyes flicking backwards (regressing) as that person re-read some words. Regressions are when you move your eyes back to re-read words and phrases.

If you have more than two regressions a page it is possible you are suffering from this poor reading habit. All of us regress in our reading such as when we daydream and suddenly wake up several paragraphs later not remembering what we have read. It is permissible, and probably necessary, to regress under these circumstances. But, be careful because regressions can become habitual.

Practice, when reading, to force yourself to move ahead and not look back under any circumstances. Use a piece of paper to mask (cover) the words you have already read as you read down the page. Be very aware that you are trying to overcome regressions as you practice forcing yourself to move on while reading. Spend a considerable amount of time on this speed reading skill. Do you regress as you read?

4) Some related poor reading habits — Reading orally (out loud) you can read at about 350 words per minute. This is top speed! If you recheck the reading rate charts in Lesson One you will find the 350 WPM is the average reading rate for most beginning students and they are reading silently. The following three poor reading habits are related to each other and the *slow* 350 WPM oral reading rate. a) Lip movement — Remember your elementary school teacher admonishing students for moving their lips when reading silently? If you say each word silently with your lips as you read, you might as well read at the slow 350 WPM oral reading rate. To find out if you move your lips when you read, get yourself some reading materials and start reading silently. Touch your finger to your lips and leave it there as you read. If you find yourself gently caressing your finger with your lips, you are guilty of lip movement while reading. Your elementary teacher was right. Don't move your lips when reading or you will be a slow

reader. Do you move your lips when you read? b) Sounding words under your breath — This saying of words in your throat usually has developed as a result of being scolded about lip movement during your school years. Your teacher could see lip movement but couldn't detect words being sounded in the throat. If you say each word you read under your breath (in your throat), you might as well be reading at the slow 350 WPM oral reading rate. Touch your finger to your adam's apple on your throat as you read. If you find your adam's apple gently vibrating, you are sounding words in your throat. Saying words under your breath while reading might have fooled the teacher but it only makes for slow reading. Do you sound words under your breath? c) Subvocalization — Somehow readers always seem to find a way to supply that gratification that only comes with oral reading or some derivation of it such as lip reading or sounding words in the throat. Subvocalization is the saying of words in your mind as you read and is related to oral reading or its variations. You *must* say words in your mind as you read or you can't recognize words or understand what you are reading. But, to say *every word* is a poor reading habit.

Subvocalization is most common and is difficult to overcome. Choose some reading materials right now and start reading. Try to say *no* as you read; for no subvocalization. The best way to overcome subvocalizing each word as you read is to read so fast (over 350 WPM) that you won't have time to subvocalize each word in your mind. Do you subvocalize every word you read? If so, you might as well be reading at the slow 350 WPM reading rate or less. Since you must subvocalize words in your mind to understand what you are reading, an answer to the question of whether or not you subvocalize is moot. Just remember that it isn't necessary to say every word in your mind to comprehend what you are reading.

5) Comprehension hang-up — Did you ever have a teacher give a reading assignment over which you would be tested? Did your parents ever threaten you with punishment if you didn't bring home a high grade in a subject that required a lot of reading such as history or literature? Things like this caused all of us to read slowly so that we would be absolutely sure to comprehend the materials. This just isn't necessary and was statistically proven by the results shown in the comprehension charts that were presented in Lesson One.

You can read much faster than you are presently doing and still have satisfactory comprehension. I know this to be true. Speed readers know it to be true. Research evidence supports the claim. You could, at this point, in a superficial way, be convinced that you can read fast with satisfactory comprehension. But, subconsciously your comprehension hang-up is saying, "If I read fast I won't comprehend." The comprehension hang-up will be the most difficult of all poor reading habits to overcome. The comprehension hang-up alone is the main reason you read slowly. You are going to have to prove to yourself that you can read fast with satisfactory comprehension through hard work and practice using the elements of speed reading presented in this book.

GOAL SETTING

1) Check your reading style to identify any of

these bad habits you might have.   2) Be
very aware of any bad reading habits you have and
make a conscious effort to correct them.
3) Understand what your bad reading habits are
and what they do to keep you from reading fast.
4) Practice the suggested activities necessary to
overcome bad reading habits. 5) By practicing,
establish the good reading habits that have been
suggested until they become an integral part of
your total reading style.

Remember to warm-up by reading, for several
minutes, a story that you have already read,
preferably from this book. You could warm-up on
the test stories that you already read in Lesson One
or Lesson Two. Force yourself to read fast. Also,
preview the test story in Lesson Three by
1) reading the title,   2) reading the first
paragraph,   3) glancing through the entire story,
and   4) reading the last paragraph. Allow yourself
30 seconds to preview the test story. Do not count
this time against the time it will take you to read the
test story.

* * * * * * * * *

RATE AND COMPREHENSION TEST

Read the following story, "Dropout." Do the
following for each of the ten Rate and
Comprehension Tests in this book:

1)   Read the story,

2)   Keep track of the time taken to read the story in
     minutes and seconds and write it down,

3) Take the comprehension test,

4) Use the chart at the end of the lesson to figure your reading rate (WPM),

5) Use the answer key at the end of the lesson to figure your comprehension level,

6) Chart your scores on the Reading Rate and Comprehension graphs on pages 177 and 178,

7) You will need a watch, or some type of timepiece, on which to keep track of the time it takes you to read the test story,

8) Think of your goal which in this lesson is to do those things that were just described in the Goal Setting portion of this lesson.

* * * * * * * * * *

* * Set your timepiece — read the story * *

DROPOUT

by Gene Gregston

Most of us, I imagine, have at some time yearned to get away from it all. It is a dream to savor. Chuck all this. Goodbye telephone. No more breakfast meetings. Scratch those command appearances on the business banquet circuit. Beachcomb in Baja California, maybe. Or find a nice little island in the Caribbean or South Pacific. A desert hideaway or a remote mountain cabin. I believe it is summed up in the plea, "Stop the world, I want to get off."

The vision may be nicer than the verity. I recently visited the place where a champion dropout found refuge from the world. The evidence remaining there and written testimony portrays an existence corresponding very little to the idyllic illusion of the escapist.

To reach the site I climbed a mile-long foot trail zig-zagging to the top of Ghost Mountain. This is a boulder-strewn, waterless, 3,200 foot mountain of the Vallecito Range in the high country at the east end of Blair Valley in Anza-Borrego Desert State Park in Southern California.

There, a writer—you would almost have guessed that, wouldn't you?—chose to live far from the madding crowd. He was Marshal South. He came to the mountain in 1931. He was forty-five. He brought a wife, Tanya, who was thirty-one. There was no Welcome Wagon. He could hardly have selected a less hospitable environment for his purpose. Incredibly they stayed fifteen years.

The mile-long trail was their only connection to the civilization they chose to leave. South wrote in 1943: "We built our home upon the summit of the mountain that rose above the canyon. It was madness, of course. No civilized beings would have deliberately sought such difficulties and hardships."

They carried everything — food, clothing, books, bedding, building materials, fuel and water — up that mountain on their backs. When it rained, South made adobe bricks. He slowly constructed, but never really completed, a house. Remains of the living room-kitchen with its massive fireplace-oven complex and one bedroom have weathered the years and vandals.

An extensive cachment and cistern system for trapping and holding water survives as testimony to the rigors of establishing life atop the mountain.

South chose a natural bowl in which to build. It provided some protection from the wind which was with them continually. Winters were bitter cold. Summers, the temperature would reach 120 degrees. Their only fuel was the wood they gathered from the brush-covered and rocky hillsides. Unless there was rain, water had to be carried up the trail from the base of the mountain. The nearest neighbor was eleven miles distant.

They kept two goats for milk. They had a burro for a while, to share the burden of pack trips up the mountain. But, there was not enough fodder for the burro so they did not keep it.

The one concession to civilization was a 1929 Model A, which South drove into Julian, a small town some twenty miles distant, to pick up supplies. Canned goods were a major staple of their diet, augmented by the produce from an undernourished garden.

South called his house "Yaquitepec," after the Yaqui Indians. Perhaps time needed no measuring, but South carved a sun dial into a stone and drove a metal center pole into it. The sun dial was re-anchored near the ruins by a conservationist group recently. It is set now for daylight savings time.

Tanya South bore three children on the mountain. And it was the only life the children knew until Rider del Sol was 12, Rudyard del Sol 8, and Victoria del Sol 6. Their mother tutored them. What they learned from nature is incalculable.

Although long hours were required in foraging for food, fuel, and water, and in building, South found time to write. Two of his novels, both westerns, were published in Great Britain. Neither was a commercial or critical success. One, *Flame of Terrible Valley*, published in 1935, is in the main branch of the San Diego Public Library. South wrote for *The Saturday Evening Post* and the *Desert Magazine.*

He described the tranquility and freedom mixed with hard toil and privation on Ghost Mountain. He contrasted the silence, scenery, and peace with the howling winds and searing heat.

Obviously, South did not escape realities by retreating into nature. He merely substituted the more harsh basic realities of life for those sophisticated ones down there beyond the valley at the foot of the mountain.

After a few years, if not less, of that life, I suspect most of us would be thankful to hear a telephone ring; we would not complain about turning down the thermostat to save energy; even having a plumber in would be a delightful expense.

South, his wife, and their three children came down off Ghost Mountain in 1946. South's weather-beaten face was framed by a shock of shoulder-length, iron-gray hair, kept back from his face with a single strand of ribbon. The children's locks were similarly long. The strain of maintaining such a rigorous lifestyle began to fray the family structure.

This was years before the hippie movement, thus the South Family's hair styles were considered somewhat strange when they appeared for a formal hearing to decide the future of the family. It was determined that the children would live with Mrs. South and she agreed to place them in a school for the first time in their lives.

At the time of the hearing Marshal South stated that his total income was forty dollars a month. Mrs. South and the children were to receive twenty-five of that amount. Such a percentage money settlement might send many men up the mountain. Or at least up the wall.

But South had seen the last of his mountain retreat. He died within two years at age 62. Not knowing, certainly, that in the years to come many of us would retrace his steps up the path on Ghost Mountain and marvel with each labored breath at the effort one man made to get away from it all.

Today, Marshal South's home on Ghost Mountain is being renovated by the California State Park Service. The building and grounds will then be maintained in a state of arrested decay.

* * * * * * * * *

IMMEDIATELY START TO ANSWER THE FOLLOWING TEN COMPREHENSION QUESTIONS. CIRCLE THE *MOST* CORRECT ANSWER. TAKE A REASONABLE AMOUNT OF TIME TO ANSWER THE QUESTIONS. YOU SHOULDN'T LOOK BACK INTO THE STORY FOR ANSWERS.

* * * * * * * * *

COMPREHENSION TEST THREE

____ 1) The name of the place where Marshal built his home is called a) Vallecitos, b) the Anza-Borrego Desert, c) Ghost Mountain.

____ 2) Marshal South and his family stayed in their home for how many years? a) 5, b) 15, c) 25.

____ 3) Marshal South wrote that anyone who would build a home where it was constructed would be considered a) uncivilized, b) foolish, c) an escapist.

___ 4) The main material from which the house was constructed was a) brick, b) wood, c) stone.

___ 5) For a time the South family used a burro to pack materials to their home but they did not keep it because a) they wanted to live as the Indians had, who had no burros, b) the wild animals kept attacking the burro, c) there wasn't enough fodder for the burro.

___ 6) Marshal South wrote two books whose theme was a) adventure, b) western, c) poetry.

___ 7) The location of the home of Marshal South required a) occasional travel to town for recreation, b) a visitation system with neighbors, c) the capture and storage of water.

___ 8) The stress of living in their secluded home eventually a) caused the South family to abandon their home, b) caused the break-up of the family, c) resulted in only Marshal South remaining in the house.

___ 9) It appears that the South Family was able to live in their remote home on an income of about a) forty dollars a month, b) fifty-five dollars a month, c) one thousand dollars a year.

___ 10) The main idea of this story seems to be a) an attempt to escape from reality, b) building a house, c) the need to maintain the home of Marshal South.

* * * * * * * * * *

CHECK YOUR ANSWERS AGAINST THE KEY ON PAGE 47
CONVERT YOUR READING TIME TO RATE USING THE CHART

ON PAGE 48 REMEMBER, ONCE YOU HAVE CONVERTED READING TIME INTO WORDS PER MINUTE (WPM) IT IS NO LONGER NECESSARY TO KEEP A RECORD OF THE READING TIME THAT IT TAKES YOU TO READ EACH STORY. CHART YOUR READING RATE (WPM) AND COMPREHENSION SCORE ON THE READING RATE GRAPH AND READING COMPREHENSION GRAPH ON PAGES 177 AND 178.

* * * * * * * * * *

PRACTICE BEFORE THE NEXT LESSON

Students have remarked that they had to try out some of the bad reading habits, even though they never had them, just to see what they were like. If you feel inclined to this, try the bad habits, discard them, and practice to overcome the bad reading habits that you do have.

Check yourself for bad reading habits. Practice the speed reading techniques necessary to overcome bad reading habits. Plan to practice thirty minutes or so daily for a week before you move on to Lesson Four. Identify and overcome the following:

1) Finger tracing — Don't move your finger across the line of words! If you must use your finger while reading, pace downward with it.

2) Don't move your head when you read — only your eyes. Have a friend check you for head movement when reading.

3) Regressions — Don't look back when you are practicing your reading. Force yourself to read on. You should try masking (covering up with paper) the words you have already read.

4) Lip movement — Saying words under your breath (sounding words in your throat) — Subvocalization. These three are related to reading

- 46 -

orally (out loud) and add up to slow reading. Check yourself using the ways suggested in Skills and Techniques and practice to overcome these bad reading habits.

5) Comprehension hang-up — To overcome a comprehension hang-up, you will need the positive attitude that you can read faster with understanding. Your weekly tests will show your reading rate progress and comprehension. Be sure that you refer to the Reading Rate Charts and Reading Comprehension Charts presented in Lesson One that prove you can read faster and still comprehend satisfactorily.

6) Review the activities under Practice Before the Next Lesson in Lesson Two.

7) Be consciously aware you are trying to overcome these poor reading habits.

8) Practice your reading using simple, columnar materials.

* * * * * * * * * *

Answers — Comprehension Test Three — 1) c, 2) b, 3) a, 4) a, 5) c, 6) b, 7) c, 8) b, 9) a, 10) a.

* * * * * * * * * *

Time	Rate—WPM	Time	Rate—WPM
1:00	1046	4:00	261
1:10	897	4:10	251
1:20	785	4:20	241
1:30	697	4:30	232
1:40	628	4:40	224
1:50	571	4:50	216
2:00	523	5:00	209
2:10	483	5:10	202
2:20	448	5:20	196
2:30	418	5:30	190
2:40	392	5:40	185
2:50	369	5:50	179
3:00	349	6:00	174
3:10	330	6:10	170
3:20	314	6:20	165
3:30	299	6:30	161
3:40	285	6:40	157
3:50	273	6:50	153

Lesson Four
SOME GENERAL ASPECTS ABOUT SPEED READING

There are certain characteristics about speed reading that are general in nature and which we will examine. As you progress through this book you might find yourself experiencing some of these characteristics:

1) Learning plateaus of both reading rate and comprehension might occur. You raise your rate and comprehension scores to a certain level and then reach a plateau (flatten out). No matter what you do you can't seem to rise above the plateau. It will just take time and practice and then your rate and/or comprehension will eventually improve.

2) To unlearn, or get rid of, poor reading habits as were identified in Lesson Three takes time. It is very easy to adhere to these poor reading habits. Over a period of time, through experimentation with good reading practices, to which you have already and will be introduced, you will be helped to overcome poor reading habits. Be sure to keep your attention on the goal of mastering these good reading practices.

3) Initially, comprehension tends to decrease as you struggle with old, poor reading practices and attempt to establish good speed reading habits. It just takes time and effort on your part to master good speed reading techniques. Comprehension will materialize as you make good speed reading habits a natural part of your reading style.

4) Speed reading students often become uncomfortable when practicing good speed reading habits. This is because you are attempting

to overcome those poor reading habits which caused you to read slowly and which were so easy to maintain. Make good speed reading skills a natural part of your reading style and this will make fast reading a comfortable process.

5) The mastery of good speed reading skills and techniques will require much repetition on your part. Spend enough time on the skills that you are to learn so they become a natural part of your reading style. Remember to review past lessons and concentrate on the skills that were presented there.

Let's examine the level of difficulty of materials that you should use which are necessary to learn speed reading techniques:

1) Any skill activity, such as speed reading, is more easily mastered using basic, simple materials. Most people would experience difficulty in learning to play the piano using musical arrangements for Van Cliburn, I think.

2) It is quite important that you *practice* your speed reading skills on materials where it is *not* essential that you remember what you read. This will allow you to concentrate on the skill to be learned without the burden of a comprehension hang-up.

3) When you have mastered the speed reading techniques which you are now and will be learning, apply them to all materials that you read.

4) Some reading materials that fall into the level of difficulty on which to practice speed reading skills and techniques would be most newspapers, weekly news magazines, and the "who dunnit" novel. The average reading level of materials prepared for mass adult consumption is about on an eighth or ninth-grade level of difficulty. So, you

can ascertain that the type of materials necessary on which to practice speed reading skills are easy to obtain.

OPENING STATEMENT

Following are some observations about aspects, not necessarily related, of speed reading:

1) It is assumed that the reader possesses an adequate vocabulary to insure the mastery of speed reading techniques and that time will not be spent on some type of vocabulary improvement during these early lessons. Vocabulary is treated in a later lesson and is not to be minimized, especially after you have learned how to read fast.

2) You must vary your rate of reading according to the type of difficulty of materials being read. Obviously you can't read technical-type materials as fast as a novel or newspaper stories. Whenever I have made this statement to speed reading students it seems to give them considerable comfort in a kind of "it's just as I thought" manner. Just don't use this as a rationalization for not reading more difficult materials with speed and comprehension. Speed reading techniques and skills can be applied to everything you read. You should always review technical materials, in the preview manner described in the Opening Statement of Lesson Two, because this will help you comprehend the message being presented. School-age students should always preview and read their assignments at least twice.

3) There is no one speed reading technique that suddenly will make you a fast reader. The skills and techniques are all interrelated and take time and practice to master. Don't hope for any one great breakthrough to speed reading mastery.

SKILLS AND TECHNIQUES

Developing the ability to use the relaxed eye fix is one of the most important speed reading skills that you will need to master. Since the time you first learned to read, you have moved your eyes from the left to the right across the line of words. This was a good way to learn to read but it causes you to use more eye fixes when reading. Satisfactory comprehension can result even when fewer eye fixes are used while reading. In the Skills and Techniques section of Lesson Two you were shown the necessity of using fewer eye fixes in order to read fast.

From now on whenever you read, your eyes should automatically look at the middle portion of the line of words on a page. Regardless of the width of the page — even if the page is a foot wide — look at the middle of the line of words! You need not stare hard and fixedly at the center of the line of words on a page but use a relaxed eye fix and just look generally into the middle of the line of words. When you start to read your eyes will move back to the left far enough to see the words there and then to the right to see the words there. This practice will help you to read phrases and groups of words. You must break yourself of having to start reading a line of words beginning at the left margin of the page!

The relaxed eye fix will help you to reduce the number of eye fixes that are necessary to read, shorten the return sweep, and help you read in phrases. Start out with the relaxed eye fix on columnar printed materials such as in a newspaper. To help you get used to looking into the middle of the line of words, get a newspaper right now. Use a ruler or straight edge and pencil in some lines on the column of words in the following manner. Imagine the horizontal lines to be words.

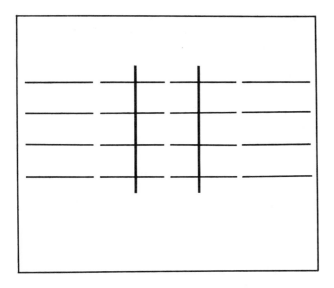

Your eyes should, using a relaxed eye fix, generally see the area between the two vertical lines. Try *not* to use eye fixes outside these lines but don't worry if you do. Place your finger or the fingertips of your hand in the middle of the column and pace downward. This will help you to remember to always use a relaxed eye fix in the center of the *printed* materials.

To develop the relaxed eye fix and to look always into the middle of the line of words will take much time and effort on your part. However, to reduce the number of eye fixes, shorten the return sweep, see phrases of words, and read down the page, you must learn to use a relaxed eye fix in order to read fast.

GOAL SETTING

Your goals this lesson are to practice the following:

1) To master the relaxed eye fix will require a great deal of practice on your part.

2) Before you do the Rate and Comprehension Test in Lesson Four, warm-up your reading style by using a story that you have previously read. Warm-up in the manner suggested in Lesson Two. Force yourself to read fast!

3) Spend 30 seconds to preview the test story in the manner described in Lesson Two.

4) During the warm-up, preview, and during the actual reading of the Rate and Comprehension Test story, try to use a relaxed eye fix. Remember that this skill will take a lot of time and practice before you can effectively use it.

5) Maintain an experimental attitude toward learning how to develop the relaxed eye fix. An experimental attitude means that you are willing to try to use those skills, like the relaxed eye fix, that are necessary to master in order to read fast.

6) From now on as you do the remaining Rate and Comprehension Tests in this book be sure to do a warm-up, a preview, and to use a relaxed eye fix.

RATE AND COMPREHENSION TEST

Read the following story, "So You're Thinking of Getting Into Backpacking?" Be sure to refer to the procedure of taking this test that was described under the Skills and Techniques section of Lesson One. Do this right now. *Do the following for this and each of the ten Rate and Comprehension Tests in this book*:

1) Read the story,

2) Keep track of the time taken to read the story in minutes and seconds and *write it down*,

3) Take the comprehension test,

4) Use the chart at the end of the lesson to figure your reading rate (WPM),

5) Use the answer key at the end of the lesson to figure your comprehension level,

6) Chart your scores on the Reading Rate and Comprehension graphs on pages 177 and 178.

7) You will need a watch, or some type of timepiece, on which to keep track of the time it takes you to read the test story,

8) Think of the speed reading goals presented in the Goal Setting portion of this lesson before you begin to read the test story.

* * Set your timepiece—read the story * *

SO YOU'RE THINKING OF GETTING INTO BACKPACKING?

by Terese M. Sutor

"How glorious a greeting the sun gives the mountains. To behold this alone is worth the pains of any excursion a thousand times over." These, the words of perhaps the pioneer of backpacking, John Muir, tend to illustrate the reason for the incredible growth of this sport in recent years.

Backpacking presents the finest, if not the only, way to experience Mother Nature in totality. It represents an attempt by man to reintegrate himself with his environment. In our modern world of jets, automobiles, and automation, we seldom have the opportunity to relax and appreciate the beauty of our world. Backpacking, which is open to almost everyone, young or old, gives us the opportunity. It is a sport in which everyone participates; there are no spectators, and it is one which everyone wins, for the rewards are many.

What are some of the prerequisites required of an individual before attempting to attain these rewarding enjoyable wilderness experiences? Foremost is the purchase of adequate and proper equipment. Although the original outlay is somewhat expensive, the backpacker-to-be will incur few additional expenses. If carefully chosen these items will, with proper care, last many years.

The three most essential pieces of equipment are shoes, backpack, and sleeping bag. In selecting these items, quality should not be compromised. Experienced hikers purchase these with the same care that a mountain climber uses in purchasing his climbing ropes. Quality equipment is durable, comfortable, usually not cheap, and requires a minimum of maintenance.

The most important purchase for a backpacker will be shoes. A good pair of trail boots is a must. In general they should be mountaineering leather or boots of good construction, ankle high, have hard toes, and a scree heel. The outer soles should be made of a composition lug sole such as Vibram Matagna which has very good wearability and incredible adhesion to smooth rock surfaces even when wet. Boots should be fully leather-lined, softly padded at the ankles, and have a pliable, high tongue. To insure a wider choice, and consequently a greater assurance of a good fit, it is strongly recommended that boots, more than any other item, be purchased in stores handling mountaineering equipment. It is also highly advisable to wear new boots at home and on several short outings before using them on more extensive trips.

Next to boots, the most important piece of equipment will be the actual backpack. The old rucksack has been superseded by modern style "packs" consisting of an aluminum (or magnesium) frame which contours itself to the body. Upon this a canvas or nylon bag is attached. The purchase of a good quality backpack is a must, for a top unit will last many years and stand up under much abuse.

Some characteristics which typify a good backpack are: 1) A fully welded frame which contours to the back; 2) Adjustable and padded shoulder straps and hip bands with a strap *not* running through the padding; 3) Adjustable back bands (bands running across the back that are attached to the frame); 4) A packbag which connects to and through the frame by means of grommets and clevic pins; 5) A suspension frame; and 6) The type that can be adjusted to one's physique. For those who do not know if they will like backpacking enough to warrant the purchase of a backpack, or do not know which brand to buy, renting from a sport shop provides a good alternative.

From the standpoint of comfort and good rest, carrying a quality sleeping bag is of great significance towards insuring an enjoyable backpacking experience. In the last few years, down-filled nylon sleeping bags have become the universal choice of backpackers. They are light, warm and compact. A good down-filled bag with two pounds of prime goose-down will weigh from three to three and one-half pounds and will keep a person warm down to about 30°F. A bag of equivalent warmth using Dacron as filler will weigh about twice as much. All bags for mountaineering should be of the mummy type in order to save weight and to maximize warmth.

Goose-down sleeping bags do not loft well when wet and they do not insulate from the ground underneath. For these reasons some backpackers prefer Dacron (DuPont) as a filler material for a sleeping bag. Besides the fact that top quality Dacron filled bags cost less than half as much as down-filled, they also retain some warmth even when wet. Furthermore, under moderate conditions, an insulating pad, such as ensolite, is not usually needed with a good Dacron bag. While Dacron bags do not pack as neatly as down bags, most are not so bulky that they cannot be carried at the bottom of the pack frame. The pros and cons of each type of material need to be carefully evaluated by each individual before a purchasing decision is made.

Other basic equipment needed by the average backpacker include the following clothing items:

1) Socks — Usually a pair of the white lightweight nylon type are worn next to the skin, followed by a heavier wool pair. Extra pairs should always be taken on a trip.

2) Pants — Levis or jeans are acceptable summertime apparel, but wool is a must during winter hiking. Roomy pants with large pockets are

very serviceable.

3) Body clothing — These should incorporate the layer system such as undershirt, wool shirt, sweater, and wind jacket. This system enables the hiker to gradually adjust to varying temperature conditions.

4) Parka — A mountain parka will serve for many years in a variety of conditions. It should be windproof and water resistant, be made of nylon or other lightweight tightly woven material, and doubled at the shoulders and main wearing points. There should be some pockets and a drawstring hood as an integral part of the parka. Do not even consider buying parkas made of rubberized or solid plastic material because they do not allow circulation of air and will be too warm. For short practice trips, any jacket will do until a decision can be made on which parka best fits an individual's needs.

5) Headgear — This should be a crushable felt type, brimmed for summer heat or a wool stocking cap type for colder weather. Since a great percentage of one's body heat is lost through an uncovered head, wearing a covering during chilly or cold weather is a considerable asset in helping one to keep warm.

6) Mittens — Large woolen mittens are much more highly recommended than gloves which, due to the separation of the fingers, are colder. Mittens can be a real blessing on a cold autumn trip, but in the summer season, generally are not needed unless altitudes above the tree line are to be encountered.

7) Long underwear — Like mittens, this article should only be carried when cold conditions are expected. Cold winds can blow hard in the high

mountains and a pair of jeans do not offer adequate protection. Long underwear can also help to provide an extra margin of warmth if your sleeping bag is inadequate for the expected temperature conditions.

8) Raingear — There are a number of useful applications of lightweight, impregnated fabrics, for protection from rain, such as rain shirts, pants, chaps, and ponchos. The latter is most practical because of its multitude of uses.

Now that the backpacker is clothed and has acquired shoes, backpack, and sleeping bag, there is another important category of equipment to be considered, and that is the "Ten Essentials." By common agreement these are certain items which a backpacker should never be without. They should be handy for use at any time although some can be packed away and used for emergencies if necessary. The "Ten" can be divided into three groups on the basis of the uses made of them. The first group is for finding one's way and includes a map of the area, compass, and a flashlight with spare batteries and bulb. The second group has articles needed for the hiker's protection such as sunglasses, spare food and water, and extra clothing, namely mittens, sweater, and jacket. Waterproof packed matches, candle or fire starter, pocket knife, and first-aid kit make up the third group. Toilet paper is jokingly referred to as an eleventh essential, and some experienced hikers feel that a whistle, which is easier to use than one's voice when calling for help, should be added as a twelfth necessity. These items are all considered to be the nucleus of one's total equipment package, and are mandatory for any outing regardless of apparent conditions and circumstances.

Another area to be considered in planning for backpacking expeditions is that of cooking equipment such as a stove, utensils, eatingware, and canteens or waterbags. For a variety of reasons a campfire is rarely used today for cooking in the wilderness. Thus the backpacker must carry his own small liquid fuel stove for cooking purposes. These stoves burn white gas, propane or alcohol, and most generate the gas by the heat of burning and do not require pumping. There are dozens of types of such stoves on the market today, and the decision as to which to buy usually rests again, on individual needs.

The length and type of trip usually dictates the size and kind of cooking utensils needed. These can range from a one-quart pot with lid to empty tin cans, aluminum foil, or merely a Sierra Cup. The cup and plate used for eating may be of aluminum or plastic, or even the handier, disposable foil dishes. Fork and spoon are useful every day; one's knife can be of the pocket variety. There are available many plastic bottles, flasks, and containers of every size to serve as canteens. Wide-mouthed translucent containers are preferred because the dirt, or even fungi that tends to collect on the inside, can easily be detected and removed. Avoid opaque containers with a very small opening. In addition a two-quart or one-gallon pliable plastic waterbag may be used to supply the camp with water and will save many a trip to the water source to fill the smaller canteens.

Finally, one last piece of equipment a backpacker must decide upon is a tent. Prominent among the reasons for having a tent is that it offers the best possible rain protection. Getting caught out in the wilderness in a cold, driving rainstorm is no fun, especially when such a storm strikes at night when one is trying to sleep! Protection from cold winds and insects are two other primary reasons for carrying a tent. In any case, one should consider a couple of factors before purchasing a tent. First, a good tent is not cheap. Expect to spend between $40 to $150 for a complete tent for backpacking. Secondly, remember that the tent means extra weight that will have to be carried. A good two-man tent weighs at least four pounds complete. That is a lot of money to spend and a lot of pounds to carry around on your back if you do not really need to carry it. However, many hikers feel the advantages of carrying and using a tent far exceed the disadvantages.

In conclusion, proper preparation and use of adequate equipment can greatly enhance one's enjoyment of a wilderness outing. Conversely, inadequate planning and use of inferior equipment can make one so miserable that he may never again return to the wilderness. So, if you're thinking of getting into backpacking, plan carefully the purchase of your necessary items. Once acquired, they should help to provide many, many, glorious "sun greetings" in your future outings.

* * * * * * * * * *

IMMEDIATELY START TO ANSWER THE FOLLOWING TEN COMPREHENSION QUESTIONS. CIRCLE THE *MOST* CORRECT ANSWER. TAKE A REASONABLE AMOUNT OF TIME TO ANSWER THE QUESTIONS. YOU SHOULDN'T LOOK BACK INTO THE STORY FOR ANSWERS.

* * * * * * * * * *

COMPREHENSION TEST FOUR

___ 1) It is suggested that backpacking is the finest, if not the only way, a) to visit a wilderness area, b) to experience the wilderness in totality, c) to travel into remote areas.

___ 2) Which of the following are the most essential pieces of equipment for backpacking? a) shoes, backpack, and food, b) shoes, backpack, and tent, c) shoes, backpack, and sleeping bag.

___ 3) Which of the following was not mentioned as an important quality when choosing a good pair of trail boots? a) lug sole, b) be ankle-high, c) lightweight.

___ 4) Regardless of the type of sleeping bag used for mountaineering, all should a) be of the mummy type, b) be down filled, c) pack down neatly.

___ 5) A mountain parka should a) be heavy to ward off the cold, b) be made of rubberized or plastic material, c) be made of lightweight, tightly woven material.

___ 6) It is best to wear clothing a) in layer-like fashion, b) that is porous to allow body heat to be trapped, c) that can be easily laundered.

___ 7) Common agreement has dictated that there are certain items which a backpacker should never be without. They are known as a) the Emergency-Survival Kit, b) the Ten Essentials, c) the Complete Backpacker's Equipment.

___ 8) When doubt exists as to the type of backpacking equipment to use, the best course to follow is a) rent all the equipment, b) consult a mountaineering store, c) join a backpacking group and take the advice of the members.

___ 9) The most prominent reason for carrying a tent is to a) provide protection from the weather, b) gain protection from the cold, c) gain relief from insect problems.

___ 10) The main thrust of this story is a) the enjoyment of backpacking, b) how to become a backpacker, c) the equipment necessary for backpacking.

* * * * * * * * * *

CHECK YOUR ANSWERS AGAINST THE KEY ON PAGE 65. CONVERT YOUR READING TIME TO RATE USING THE CHART ON PAGE 66. REMEMBER, ONCE YOU HAVE CONVERTED READING TIME INTO WORDS PER MINUTE (WPM) IT IS NO LONGER NECESSARY TO KEEP A RECORD OF THE READING TIME THAT IT TAKES YOU TO READ EACH STORY. CHART YOUR READING RATE (WPM) AND COMPREHENSION SCORE ON THE READING RATE GRAPH AND READING COMPREHENSION GRAPH ON PAGES 177 AND 178.

* * * * * * * * * *

PRACTICE BEFORE THE NEXT LESSON

1) Find some reading materials that are written in a columnar fashion. Draw some vertical lines through the column of words as was shown in the Skills and Techniques section of this lesson.

2) Softly fix your eyes on the words between the vertical lines and read down the page.

3) Concentrate on the relaxed eye fix skill but don't stare fixedly at the middle of the line of words.

4) Be relaxed in your study area where you do your lessons and look at the middle portion of the line of words.

5) Practice a great deal in order to master the relaxed eye fix.

* * * * * * * * * *

Answers — Comprehension Test Four — 1) b, 2) c), 3) c, 4) a, 5) c, 6) a, 7) b, 8) b, 9) a, 10) c.

* * * * * * * * * *

Time	Rate—WPM	Time	Rate—WPM
1:00	1921	5:40	339
1:10	1647	5:50	329
1:20	1441	6:00	320
1:30	1281	6:10	312
1:40	1153	6:20	303
1:50	1048	6:30	296
2:00	960	6:40	288
2:10	887	6:50	281
2:20	823	7:00	274
2:30	768	7:10	268
2:40	720	7:20	261
2:50	678	7:30	256
3:00	640	7:40	251
3:10	607	7:50	245
3:20	576	8:00	240
3:30	549	8:10	235
3:40	524	8:20	231
3:50	510	8:30	226
4:00	480	8:40	222
4:10	461	8:50	217
4:20	443	9:00	213
4:30	427	9:10	209
4:40	412	9:20	206
4:50	397	9:30	202
5:00	384	9:40	199
5:10	372	9:50	195
5:20	360	10:00	192
5:30	349		

Lesson Five
GOOD SPEED READING
PRACTICES

An interesting circumstance that occurs with the eyes when reading is known as a retinal image. When your eyes see anything, objects, symbols, words, phrases, etc., the image appears on the back or retina of the eye. A large nerve attached to the retina connects with the brain and informs you of what you are seeing. Readers are generally not aware of the retinal image.

Do you remember subliminal advertising on TV? Advertising messages were being flashed onto the TV screen for only a split second. The viewer was totally unaware that a commercial message had been "sneaked" into his brain. However, the retinas of the eyes had perceived the image and the brain registered the commercial message. The federal government decided that the method was so insidious to the viewer that it was outlawed as an advertising method.

The retinal image is important to any reader because it is fundamental to comprehension. To the speed reader it means that you can read very fast, seemingly somewhat unaware of the words and phrases being read, but your eyes and brain combine to comprehend the message of the written materials. All this may occur rather unconsciously on your part.

The retinal image might appear to be somewhat mystical at this point but devices designed to aid in word and word-phrase recognition have been around for a long time. A number of mechanical devices to assist readers to retain a retinal image for a longer period of time are generally described as providing tachistoscopic training. Such tachistoscopic machines, etc., are available from educational supply houses. Some devices are quite functional such as those used by the military to recognize planes and ship silhouettes through quick recognition. More sophisticated machines help train readers to keep images they have seen in such a manner to allow the brain to interpret what is being viewed even though the eyes have moved onto words further on in the story.

I am unable to present a mechanical device in this book that would help you graphically to discern just what a retinal image is. You might be able to obtain a tachistoscopic device to assist you to develop your ability to maintain an image on the retina of your eye and to acquire the subsequent resulting benefits of comprehension. Such devices certainly aren't totally necessary to fast reading but only serve as a tool. Forcing yourself to read fast by seeing phrases of words or masking (covering lines of words you have already read) will help you to develop the retinal image and to comprehend more fully what you read. Remember that the retinal image is present in all reading and that satisfactory comprehension can result even though much faster reading rates are being achieved.

A type of vision constantly used which results in depth perception is peripheral vision. This constitutes an ability to see to either side even when looking straight forward. Humans aren't generally too aware of peripheral or side vision. But, it is significant because it allows you to read groups or phrases of words. To test your peripheral vision place your hands to the side and toward the back of your head and slowly move them forward until you can recognize their presence. Activities designed to help use peripheral vision to develop your ability to read phrases and groups of words will be presented later on in this lesson.

OPENING STATEMENT

Learning speed reading techniques is essentially a mechanical process. It is definitely not an intellectual exercise. This was mentioned briefly in Lesson Three and merits further examination at this time. To read with speed it is necessary to rid yourself of poor reading habits and to establish good ones through mechanical repetition and practice.

Shortly, some good speed reading practices are going to be examined by the reader. To aid in the development and mastery of speed reading techniques: 1) Develop a habitual reading pattern that you follow when practicing your speed reading techniques. Set aside a time and place to regularly practice. 2) With practice, speed reading techniques will become an integral part of your reading style.

SKILLS AND TECHNIQUES

In this lesson you are going to learn about and be working on 16 good reading practices which are totally important to development of speed reading skills. To master these 16 skills will require tremendous concentration and effort on your part. Some of the techniques have been discussed in earlier lessons:

1) Reducing the number of eye fixes necessary to read a line of words. This was touched upon in Lesson Two and treated more extensively (the relaxed eye fix) in Lesson Four. By this time you

have probably partially mastered the reduction of eye fixes when reading by using the techniques suggested earlier. It would profit you to review these earlier lessons.

2) Reducing the length of the return sweep. Again, you have probably mastered this reading skill that was presented in Lesson Two. Remember to use a relaxed eye fix when looking at the middle of the line of words to be read. Don't allow your eyes to return to the left margin of the page or travel to the right margin of the page when reading. Review this skill in Lesson Two.

3) Be relaxed and comfortable while you practice and learn your speed reading skills and techniques.

4) Practice your lessons in a comfortable and familiar place each time as you do your speed reading work. Certainly this isn't always possible to do, but set aside a place to practice and use this same place as much as is practical.

5) The following item is absolutely and completely important when practicing speed reading. Be aware that you are performing the act of reading while learning speed reading techniques — not what you are reading — but that you are reading! This most important action will help your mind to focus on the reading skills to be mastered. Remember the first grader who came home near Christmas time and proudly announced his ability to read a story? How exciting an event for the child. Yet what the child was reading wasn't nearly as important to him as the fact that he was reading. From that point on a person tends to pay more attention to what he is reading rather than how he is reading. To help you concentrate upon and master the skills of speed reading, return to

that basic premise of awareness of the act of reading. It will help you focus on the skills to be learned.

6) How important it is to read with the purpose in mind of developing a specific or combination of reading skills! Don't be concerned with what you are reading but that you are practicing to develop skills and techniques of speed reading.

7) Use simple reading materials while learning speed reading techniques. This was touched upon in Lesson Four. A person's ego can become involved when using simple (average) reading materials is beneath his or her intelligence. The fear can emerge that the transference of speed reading skills cannot be made to more difficult reading materials. Mechanical skills, which make up speed reading, are best learned starting on a basic level. With mastery a person can effectively perform on a more proficient level while reading more difficult materials.

8) The relaxed eye fix was covered extensively in Lesson Four. Always use this skill while speed reading.

9) Increasing the eye span enables you to see groups and phrases of words while reading. You must read phrases of words to read fast. Earlier in this lesson peripheral vision was discussed and is a necessary action in order to read phrases of words. Specific materials on which to practice are included under the Practice Before the Next Lesson portion of this lesson.

10) Recognizing phrases of words when reading is a very natural function. The structure of sentences consists of phrases of words which due to their nature can be read in a very natural manner. Look for word phrases in the printed

materials that you read and be aware of them as you practice your speed reading. The underlined parts of the previous sentence are illustrations of word phrases.

11) Read down the column of words — *not across*. Start with a relaxed eye fix in the middle of the column of words and practice reading downward. Your eyes will automatically use enough eye fixes to read the printed words in the column. To help you to master this technique draw two lines down a column of printed materials in the following fashion:

Use a relaxed eye fix between the two lines and read downward.

12) Use your finger, hand, or other object to help you pace *down* the column of printed material. Personally, I feel that once you have learned to read down the page that you shouldn't use a "crutch" such as a finger while reading. But it is sometimes helpful to use a pacing device while learning speed reading skills. Under no circumstances should you use your finger, etc., to trace under the words *across* the page!

13) Get rid of bad reading habits. These poor habits were described in Lesson Three and practices were prescribed to help rid yourself of them. Review these bad reading habits by returning to Lesson Three. Assess your gains in overcoming any of the poor reading habits that you may have had.

14) Using the skimming reading technique will be covered in Lesson Seven.

15) Don't be overly concerned with

comprehension as you practice your reading skills because your fear of not understanding what you read will interfere with the skill that you are trying to master. This is the "comprehension hang-up" which was discussed in the Skills and Techniques portion of Lesson Three.

16) *Force yourself to read faster!* To my knowledge most authorities in the speed reading field agree on this practice. Find a story right now in a newspaper or magazine. Force yourself to read as fast as you can. This activity will make you uncomfortable and you will worry about comprehension. Never mind; force yourself to read faster. Specific techniques to aid you in forcing yourself to read faster will be advanced in future lessons. With effort and practice on your past, fast reading will become a natural and comfortable part of your reading style.

GOAL SETTING

Your goal is to understand and master the good speed reading techniques presented in this lesson. This is a rather prodigious undertaking on your part. Spend considerable time practicing on the techniques advanced in this lesson while reading your practice materials. Be sure to have a specific skill or skills in mind while practicing.

In this lesson you will embark upon a new method to use when reading the Rate and Comprehension Test. Set a goal to read the story in a certain *number of words per minute* or within a certain *amount of time*. To assist you in setting a reading rate or time goal, refer to the results you have achieved on past stories that are recorded on the Reading Rate Graph on page 177. Set a rate or time goal that is higher than what you have previously done and don't be afraid to set it high as students tend to underestimate their ability to read fast. Suppose your reading rate has been averaging about 350 WPM. You might set a goal to read at the rate of 500 WPM on a story. If your goal is stated in time a similar application can be made. Whichever of the two ways you decide to use for goal setting purposes, stay with it through the test story in this lesson. Then, on the test story in Lesson Six, use the other way. You will be able to compare the effectiveness of the two methods, thereby determining which goal setting method, time or WPM, is more useful to you.

Warm-up on a Rate and Comprehension Test story that you have previously read. Be sure to force yourself to read fast. Remember to preview the test story in this lesson.

* * * * * * * * * *

RATE AND COMPREHENSION TEST

Read the following story, "Brunch For The Bunch — An Alternative Type of Entertaining." Be sure to refer to the procedure for taking this test that was described under the Skills and Techniques section of Lesson One. Do this right now. *Do the following for this and each of the ten Rate and Comprehension Tests in this book:*
1) Read the story,

2) Keep track of the time taken to read the story in minutes and seconds and *write it down,*

3) Take the comprehension test,

4) Use the chart at the end of the lesson to figure your reading rate (WPM),

5) Use the answer key at the end of the lesson to figure your comprehension level,

6) Chart your scores on the Reading Rate and Comprehension graphs on pages 177 and 178.

7) You will need a watch, or some type of timepiece, on which to keep track of the time it takes you to read the test story,

8) Think of the speed reading goals presented in the Goal Setting portion of this lesson before you begin to read the test story.

* * * * * * * * * *

* * Set your timepiece — read the story * *

BRUNCH FOR THE BUNCH — AN ALTERNATIVE TYPE OF ENTERTAINING

by George Class

How many times have you thought about having a dinner party or planned to entertain a group of friends, business associates, or club members, and have just never gotten around to it? How many times have you thought about showing your appreciation to those people who have had you over for dinner or a party and you neglected to reciprocate? Many times, I'm sure. You probably thought about it, but for one reason or another you just kept putting it off. Your reasons were probably varied. If you are married, maybe your wife or husband didn't want to be bothered. Maybe you felt that it would be too difficult a task and that you couldn't cope with such an undertaking. Perhaps you came up with some other reasons for not entertaining like: I don't have the nerve, I don't have the necessary serving pieces or table settings, it's too expensive, I can't handle large, formal sit-down dinners, or some other justification that may have crossed your mind. Any of these could interfere with your success in entertaining larger groups of people.

All of that apprehension about having large-group get-togethers can be changed to a more positive viewpoint. Forget those large formal dinner parties and use the brunch idea as the alternative to easy, carefree, uncomplicated entertaining. Married couples, children, friends, or singles will find brunch (a late-late breakfast) can be one of the easiest, informal and relaxing ways of servicing a group of people. Whether you want to entertain a small or large group, you will discover (after you try it) that brunch is an elegant and easy way of entertaining.

Whatever your reasons for entertaining, brunch can be used for many occasions. You may want to have a Sunday brunch for your friends. The Christmas holiday season is a great time for friendship. Don't forget these special holidays observed by your ethnic friends. Easter, the Fourth of July, Mother's Day, Thanksgiving, birthdays, before sporting events — the list is unlimited. Whatever the occasion, when you want to have a group of people at your home, why not use the brunch approach?

Now that you have had your introduction to brunch as an alternative type of entertaining, you will need to develop a plan and put it into action.

One of the easiest methods is to make a commitment to yourself that you are going to undertake a brunch. Plan the date, invite your guests (tell them it is informal), and then think about the menu and decor. You will find that the most difficult decision was to make the commitment to have the brunch in the first place. From that point on, it seems as though everything falls into place, ready or not. Your guests will never know how many times you changed your menu or how you fretted about this and that. The main concern is that when the time and date arrive, you had better be ready because your guests will be!

The following are some ideas that you should consider when putting your brunch plan into action.

What to serve — If you have a collection of recipes or cookbooks, you will have little difficulty in creating and preparing a menu that will permit you to spend a lot of time with your guests. Simplicity and advance preparation are key factors. Here are some serving suggestions:

a) Fruit salad — prepared early in the morning or the day before.

b) Biscuits or muffins — can be baked ahead of time and reheated at the last minute or baked just before serving.

c) Casseroles — can be assembled early in the day and timed and baked to perfection. You can create many casserole dishes with eggs.

d) Meats — use meats that can be pan fried quickly or warmed in the oven. Use ham slices or sausage. Stay away from bacon because it is too much trouble.

e) Vegetables — use seasonal vegetables like broccoli, asparagus spears, or mushrooms.

f) Desserts — your favorite homemade dessert or frozen cakes, tarts, strudel, or pastries.

Remember that your menu can be as simple or as substantial as you may wish. The later your brunch, the more you should rely on the more substantial entrees.

At what time should the guests arrive? — An acceptable time would be 10:00 a.m. Plan to serve your brunch around 11:00 a.m. One hour of socializing is adequate. Two more hours for dining and conversation is sufficient. Regardless of the time that you feel is appropriate, set your target hour and stick to it.

Beverages — Chilled fruit and vegetable juices can be prepared in creative ways. Juices garnished with fresh fruit or vegetables (e.g. a celery stick) are quite appropriate. Serve easily prepared beverages and shy away from complicated blender prepared drinks. Serve your guests the first drink and then let them help themselves to the second one. It is best to have a selection of beverages. Some guests may prefer an early cup of coffee rather than a cold drink.

Planning menus — It pays to spend a lot of time planning what you are going to serve. Serve entrees that require a minimum of bother or last-minute preparation time. If you can serve entrees with a minimum of last-minute preparation, your guests will be impressed as to how you could put together such a superb brunch and yet be able to mix casually with guests and then, out of nowhere announce, "Brunch is served."

How to serve — buffet, sit down, or TV trays — It partially depends on the type of entree being served. You can either have your guests serve themselves from a buffet or you can serve the main entree from the kitchen. Whatever method is used, get the food hot and maintain it at the desired temperature. The layout of your residence will determine, to an extent, how and what method you will use for serving. If you do serve buffet style, and there is inadequate table space, be sure to provide TV trays or lap trays for your guests. There is nothing more frustrating than trying to perform a balancing act with plates, cups, and silverware on your lap.

Who is on duty? — The host and hostess are both on duty. Don't deputize your guests. If you feel that you may need some help with last-minute preparations, ask a very close friend whom you know would not mind helping you out. If one of your guests offers his help, decline unless you are in dire need of assistance.

Table decorations — It all depends on the occasion. If you are having your brunch during the Christmas holidays you probably have a nice selection of decorations that you can use. You can decorate according to the season or holiday near or on the brunch date. If you have difficulty in selecting a theme, you can always use flowers. Don't overlook your own creativity — it may surprise you!

Indoor or outdoor dining — If you have a patio or outdoor dining area, and weather permitting, by all means plan to dine outdoors. There is nothing more pleasurable than outdoor dining combined with good food and enjoyable company. Be prepared with an alternative plan if the weather is uncooperative.

Smokers versus non-smokers — With so much emphasis today on smoking, try to group your guests together on a smoking and non-smoking basis. Your guests will appreciate it. If you are a non-smoker, try to be as considerate as possible of those guests who do smoke, since the brunch is for a relatively short period of time.

THE ODDS-N-ENDS HINT DEPARTMENT — Following are some ideas:

Omelets — Add a tablespoon of cold water to every three eggs to make them fluffy. Eggs should always be at room temperature before using them in omelets and scrambled eggs. Allow at least an hour after they come from the refrigerator.

Sausage — When you are preparing sausage links for a crowd, you can bake pork sausage links in a pre-heated oven at 400 degrees for about 20 minutes, turning them once to brown. Use a shallow, rimmed pan. Another sausage tip is to boil link sausages for 10 to 15 minutes and drain them in a colander. This will remove most of the grease from the sausage. After the sausages are cool, they can be refrigerated or frozen until needed. When ready to serve, they can be fried until slightly browned.

Warm Plates — Place your serving plates in the dishwasher and set the dishwasher on the dry cycle. Presto! Nice warm plates!

Food warmer — You can also use your warmed dishwasher cycle to keep those muffins, rolls, or whatever, warm if your oven is being used to cook or heat other foods.

Sample menus — Your menu plans are unlimited and can be coordinated to the foods, fruits, and vegetables that are in season. Don't overlook frozen foods; they are time savers.

Consider:

Menu No. 1
Fresh fruit salad
Quiche lorraine
Asparagus spears
Canadian bacon or ham slices
Muffins
Pastry, tarts, cheese cake
Coffee, tea, or milk

Menu No. 2
Lime sherbet with frozen or fresh fruits
Baked eggs
Sausage
Broccoli pieces
Rolls or muffins
Coffee, tea, or milk

Well, that's it! Now that you have been introduced to brunch as an alternative type of entertaining, plan a brunch and make that commitment to yourself, and your friends, today. Get those invitations in the mail or telephone your friends. Put to use those ideas and hints that were presented and you will agree (after you get all of those compliments from your guests) that brunch for the bunch can be an elegant and easy way of entertaining your friends, club members, or business associates.

* * * * * * * * *

IMMEDIATELY START TO ANSWER THE FOLLOWING TEN COMPREHENSION QUESTIONS. CIRCLE THE *MOST* CORRECT ANSWER. TAKE A REASONABLE AMOUNT OF TIME TO ANSWER THE QUESTIONS. YOU SHOULDN'T LOOK BACK INTO THE STORY FOR ANSWERS.

* * * * * * * * *

COMPREHENSION TEST FIVE

___ 1) Probably the main reason that people haven't undertaken the giving of a brunch is a) they hadn't considered this type of entertaining, b) they have inadequate facilities for entertaining, c) it is too early in the day to entertain.

___ 2) Which of the following was not mentioned as an occasion for giving a brunch? a) a holiday, b) before sporting events, c) at the week's end.

___ 3) Probably the most difficult decision that will need to be made when planning a brunch will be a) who to invite, b) the commitment to have the brunch, c) planning the menu.

___ 4) When planning what to serve, simplicity and advance preparation will a) allow you to spend a lot of time with your guests, b) practically assure the success of the brunch, c) make giving a brunch an easy affair.

___ 5) The later the brunch a) the more your guests will appreciate the food, b) the more time you will have for preparation, c) the more substantial the menu should be.

___ 6) Regarding beverages, the author feels that a) it is best to shy away from the complicated blender-type drinks, b) a single "punch-bowl" type beverage is best, c) guests should help themselves.

___ 7) Buffet, sit down, or TV trays are all acceptable ways of serving food but, to a large extent, the thing that dictates which method to use is a) the personal preference of the host, b) the layout of your residence, c) the type of invited guests.

___ 8) Omelets will be a failure if a) eggs are prepared at room temperature, b) eggs are used directly from the refrigerator, c) eggs are mixed with water.

___ 9) Which of the following is probably the most important when serving the food to the guests? a) Make sure each guest has equal portions of food, b) Make sure each guest is comfortably seated before serving, c) Serve the food at the proper temperature.

___ 10) Generally, this story is about a) how to give a brunch, b) the food and decor involved when serving a brunch, c) helpful hints about serving a brunch.

* * * * * * * * * *

CHECK YOUR ANSWERS AGAINST THE KEY ON PAGE 86 CONVERT YOUR READING TIME TO RATE USING THE CHART ON PAGE 87 REMEMBER, ONCE YOU HAVE CONVERTED READING TIME INTO WORDS PER MINUTE (WPM) IT IS NO LONGER NECESSARY TO KEEP A RECORD OF THE READING TIME THAT IT TAKES YOU TO READ EACH STORY. CHART YOUR READING RATE AND COMPREHENSION SCORE ON THE READING RATE GRAPH AND READING COMPREHENSION GRAPH ON PAGES 177 AND 178.

* * * * * * * * * *

PRACTICE BEFORE THE NEXT LESSON

The list of good reading practices presented in the Skills and Techniques section of this lesson is lengthy. A considerable amount of time will need to be spent on practicing these skills. Take each individual good reading skill and consciously be aware of it as you practice reading. Choose simple, columnar materials on which to read and practice. A newspaper or news magazine would be fine to use. Know and master these good reading skills through practice and repetition.

While you are practicing the good reading techniques try not to be so concerned with comprehension. Such concern can divert your concentration and distract the mental attitude that is necessary to consciously practice and master that skill. Force yourself to read fast; use a relaxed eye fix; read down the page of words; and set your goal high.

Following are two practice activities to help develop your eye span. The first activity is a three-digit number drill. Concentrate your relaxed eye fix on the center digit and read it as a three-place number. Read down the column and don't peek at either side digit but see them with your peripheral vision.

7	8	9
4	2	3
1	9	7
6	7	5
9	4	2
1	5	5
8	6	7
5	9	1
2	1	8
3	8	4
6	4	8
2	2	1
8	7	8
3	4	5
5	7	2
5	5	1
9	1	4
2	9	6
4	1	1
3	1	2

Practice the following three-word-phrase drill to aid in developing your eye span. Concentrate your relaxed eye fix on the center word and say the three-word phrase. Read down the column and try not to peek at either side word.

FLY	THE	FLAG
RED	WHITE	BLUE
DOWN	THE	HATCH
HOME	SWEET	HOME
SAN	DIEGO	ZOO
FIRST	SECOND	THIRD
PURPLE	PEOPLE	EATERS
SHOOT	THE	RAPIDS
TOM	DICK	HARRY
HOLE	IN	ONE
WAIT	A	MINUTE
DO	YOUR	THING
BLOOD	SWEAT	TEARS
MILES	PER	HOUR
HOLD	THAT	TIGER
OLD	KING	COLE
CLAIM	TO	FAME
WHIP	INFLATION	NOW
SAVE	THE	CHILDREN
CLIMB	THE	WALLS

* * * * * * * * * *

Answers — Comprehension Test Five — 1) a, 2) c, 3) b, 4) a, 5) c, 6) a, 7) b, 8) b, 9) c, 10) a.

* * * * * * * * * *

Time	Rate—WPM	Time	Rate—WPM
1:00	1628	5:30	296
1:10	1395	5:40	287
1:20	1221	5:50	279
1:30	1085	6:00	271
1:40	977	6:10	264
1:50	888	6:20	257
2:00	814	6:30	250
2:10	751	6:40	244
2:20	698	6:50	238
2:30	651	7:00	233
2:40	611	7:10	227
2:50	575	7:20	222
3:00	543	7:30	217
3:10	514	7:40	212
3:20	488	7:50	207
3:30	465	8:00	203
3:40	444	8:10	199
3:50	425	8:20	195
4:00	407	8:30	192
4:10	391	8:40	188
4:20	376	8:50	184
4:30	362	9:00	181
4:40	349	9:10	178
4:50	337	9:20	174
5:00	326	9:30	171
5:10	315	9:40	168
5:20	305	9:50	166

Lesson Six
STORY PARTS AND GOAL SETTING

In previous lessons you have, in numerous instances, been exposed to reading rates expressed in words per minute (WPM). How high should your reading rate goal be? I've had students achieve very high reading rates and you probably know of other similar high reading rates bordering on the "fantastic." These high reading rates certainly are achieved and students have had satisfactory comprehension. However, don't be a slave to high reading rates. Ego can become involved and the reading rate becomes more important than mastering the good reading techniques that are necessary to your establishment of a lasting speed reading style which will allow you to read with speed and satisfactory comprehension. Remember that your purpose is to learn to read fast, effectively, and with comprehension.

Questions will arise regarding adjustment of your reading rate according to the kinds of materials being read. Let's get it straight right now! You must read certain materials more slowly than others. Some materials can be read faster than others for various reasons. 1) Newspapers, magazines, and novels can be read fastest because generally people are attempting to keep abreast of current events or are reading for pleasure and such reading doesn't require a testable amount of recall. However, don't use this as a rationalization to read only certain materials fast. All materials can be read faster than most people realize. 2) Technical materials slow down the reading rate due to their factual content and will take the most time to read.

Carefully previewing such materials (first mentioned in Lesson Two), which you do before taking each Rate and Comprehension Test, is most helpful and should *always* be applied when "setting up" technical materials to be read. 3) When reading materials that you *must know*, preview them and read them more than once!

OPENING STATEMENT

Novels, stories, fiction stories, and even some non-fiction stories, generally contain five identifiable parts. An ability to recognize these parts can help you to effectively preview a story and will aid your comprehension of the story. The five parts generally occur in the following sequence: 1) *Setting.* This is where the story takes place. Often you not only get clues about the place setting of the story but also the time of day or month or period of time historically. These things often occur quite early in the story. 2) *Characters* are often introduced early in the story. Look for age, sex, physical descriptions, occupations, and personality characteristics. Of course, characters can and do appear throughout the entire story. 3) *Action* is simply all those things that characters do and become involved in throughout the entire story. 4) *Climax.* This is the most important part of the story. It is the plot or what the story is all about. The characters and their actions build to the climax which occurs near the end of the story. 5) *Conclusion.* This part of the story describes what happens to the characters and closes out the action. The conclusion is short and finishes the story quickly.

SKILLS AND TECHNIQUES

Americans are generally goal oriented and respond in a positive manner to attain goals that we set for ourselves. We are going to examine some goals that will help you become a faster reader and understand what you read. 1) When doing the Rate and Comprehension Test, always set a goal to read the story in either a certain amount of time or words per minutes (WPM) as was suggested in Lesson Five. 2) Establish a set routine each time you practice your speed reading techniques. Choose your favorite reading place, practice your reading skills, set your goals, take the Rate and Comprehension Test and practice the exercises suggested in Practice Before the Next Lesson section of lesson. The security of such a routine will assist you in mastering speed reading skills.

There are three goals that you will always face when doing your speed reading lessons: 1) Reading against time. You read against time whenever you take a Rate and Comprehension Test. Psychologically, humans will perform tasks differently from normal when faced with a time factor. 2) Reading toward a goal. Always establish a reading goal and have the goal in mind when mastering your speed reading techniques. For example, you may choose a time goal to read your story or your goal might be to practice a speed reading technique such as using your finger to help your reading down a page of words. 3) Improving upon your past record of performance. Always refer to your Reading Rate Record Graph and Reading Comprehension Graph on pages 177 and 178 to help you set a goal of improving upon your past performance. Do this each time you take your Rate and Comprehension Test.

GOAL SETTING

Before you do the Rate and Comprehension Test you will need to perform two distinct actions and do a third one while actually reading the story:

1) As a way to preview the story look for the following five items: a Setting, Characters, Action, Climax, and a Conclusion. Keep within the 30 second preview time limitation.

2) In Lesson Five you set a goal to read the Rate and Comprehension Test Story in a certain number of *words per minute* or within a certain amount *of time*. Whichever of the two ways you chose last time, do the opposite one in Lesson Six. To assist you in setting your time or rate goal, check the results you have achieved on past stories by referring to the Reading Rate Graph on page 177.

3) The following reading method is extremely important! Your goal will be to read the Rate and Comprehension Test story in the following way. Use a relaxed eye fix and read down the page of printed material reading all, or most all, the words *just as fast as you can possibly force yourself to read.* Stay with this method throughout the entire test story.

In Lesson Seven you will read the Rate Comprehension Test story using a skimming method. After that you will be able to compare that method of reading with the method of reading you will use in Lesson Six. Warm-up on a Rate and Comprehension Test previously read and force yourself to read fast. Remember to preview the test story in the manner just described in the Goal Setting portion of this lesson.

* * * * * * * * * *

RATE AND COMPREHENSION TEST

Read the following story, "Travel Today — A New Personal Age of Discovery." *Do the following for each of the ten Rate and Comprehension Tests in this book:*

1) Read the story,

2) Keep track of the time taken to read the story in minutes and seconds and *write it down,*

3) Take the comprehension test,

4) Use the chart at the end of the lesson to figure your reading rate (WPM),

5) Use the answer key at the end of the lesson to figure your comprehension level,

6) Chart your scores on the Reading Rate and Comprehension graphs on pages 177 and 178,

7) You will need a watch, or some type of timepiece, on which to keep track of the time it takes you to read the test story,

8) Think of your goal which in this lesson is to do those things that were just described in the Goal Setting portion of this lesson.

* * * * * * * * *

* * Set your timepiece — read the story * *

TRAVEL TODAY — A NEW PERSONAL AGE OF DISCOVERY

by Robert L. Coath

Long distance travel today is possible for many of the world's people. Travel is most prevalent and available in societies with moderate to high economic development and where personal freedom of mobility is held in high esteem. Today's travel in vehicles of fast speed and reasonable safety has spawned a new "Age of Discovery." This is primarily due to the technological genius of western civilization. While the desire for distant travel is evident in some early writings, today's travel explosion is modern and western. The attempts of men who sought discovery through travel are legend and in a sense we live in an age where the mythical "flying carpet" has become the reality of earlier dreams.

To the seasoned traveler, traveling is a skill that must be learned in order to obtain the greatest pleasures of discovery. On one hand, discovering the varied ways of life as practiced by people of different cultures generates satisfaction. On the other hand, to view the vast array of scenic beauty that exists on this planet is most pleasurable. Through travel one can enhance his personal awareness and develop understanding about other people by observing, even though it be of short duration, interactions between people and the relationship of people and their environment. It is remarkable that cultural differences are as varied as the colors that exist in the rock strata upon which man walks.

For the novice traveler some words of caution are in order. Having a desire to travel is just not good enough. To proceed to make a long journey without proper preparation may not allow achievement of the rewards of that trip in spite of all the effort expended in making the excursion in the first place. To illustrate, a young man developed a desire to visit Europe. One day he informed his parents of his plans to immediately depart for Europe. He traveled from California to New York City where he purchased an off season airline ticket to Germany. When the airliner landed in Frankfurt, Germany, the weather was cold with drizzling rain. He hadn't calculated on the decided difference in weather between California and Central Europe. In a strange land, with clothes fit only for a dissimilar climate, he developed some vague ideas about getting part-time work to help pay for some warm clothing and for his up-keep. Unable to read German and understanding the culture even less, he had no acquaintances who could take him in and offer some help or orientation.

The young man walked out of the airport into the gray rainy day. Wet and disillusioned, he walked the streets hoping to see something that might transform his growing sense of disappointment into something positive that would justify his efforts up to that time. Surmising that he had trapped himself into a less-than-desirable situation, he spent several dreary days in Frankfurt, returned to the airport, and hopped the first airplane home.

The aforementioned trip actually took place. That young man went to Europe and what a lesson he learned. That trip may have caused him such personal frustrations that any desire for future travel was killed or at least dulled. It should have been an interesting trip, and it could have been, if only our young friend had taken some precautionary action in thinking out what he was trying to accomplish. Obviously, the lesson to be learned is that early and complete planning should precede any incursion into trip taking. The following are some suggestions to use when preparing for a long-distance journey.

Suggestion #1 — For the traveler to prepare, find out facts and information about the place being visited and try to determine what experiences are desired or which ones are most likely to be experienced. Interest in travel can be stimulated merely by becoming involved with ideas that center around a journey and the travel techniques necessary to achieve it.

Most people have personal friends who have traveled. Have you ever known one who wasn't willing to tell you about the worthwhile events that occurred and which things to avoid? Listen to their tale and be sure to ask lots of questions; literally pick their brains. Other worthwhile sources of information include travel articles that are found in newspapers and magazines; viewing travel programs on television; and attending travel lectures presented to the public by professional travelers.

One's personal knowledge about places can be increased by using materials readily available in a library or by purchasing inexpensive paperback travel books that contain current data that are helpful to know while traveling. Free travel materials can often be obtained from the public relations departments of large airlines and shiplines. Foreign consulates often provide materials in an effort to stimulate travel to their countries. Keep in mind that a large part of a trip consists of planning and the resulting anticipation leading up to the journey itself.

Suggestion #2 — The second suggestion deals with those things the traveler needs to know in securing transportation to a prime arrival point and one of departure. This will require careful examination of many schedules dealing with flights or sailing times and areas of boarding. Most flights and sailing bookings require advance confirmation with money deposits paid. In making such reservations it is also best to prepare some contingency plans in case prearranged schedules cannot be kept. Also, what would happen to the money paid for the return trip if the traveler became ill and had to abort the remainder of the package tour? Things like this happen and the traveler should have an answer to such a problem.

Plans need to be made as to just how and where lodgings can be found. If the airplane should arrive in a foreign city very late at night could accommodations be found for the remainder of the night? The writer can speak from experience that airport lounges are not comfortable places in which to get a restful sleep. Imagine landing at a foreign airport late at night, going through their customs, and then finding out that no hotel, etc., would take your money simply because it is the wrong kind. It is best to have some currency of the country being visited on the traveler's person upon landing. Money talks in any language — the proper kind of money that is. Generally, the traveler who has secured adequate funds can make arrangements for lodging on arrival. This is especially true when journeying to a large modern city. However, arriving at some remote city, far off the beaten path, with no prior reservations having been made is taking more than a reasonable chance. It is a sure-fire setup for troubles to begin almost at once.

Suggestion #3 — The novice traveler should never risk a solo trip to some remote place. Whenever visiting such areas always rely on the services offered through a bonafide package tour. Agents from such companies will arrange transportation to the locale to be visited, will provide for reasonably edible food, and secure lodging that should be relatively free from insects, snakes, or other dangerous animals such as lions or panthers. This is really no joking matter. Such things need to be considered when on a safari or exotic-type trips.

Not too long ago the writer was making an extensive tour, in a car caravan, through the heartland of Holy India. The drive was long and the roads, while not particularly occupied with cars, were often crowded with people and animals. India not only possesses one of the earth's huge populations but also has the greatest number of domestic cattle in the world. Seemingly, most cattle walk at their leisure and often block the flow of traffic by lying down in the middle of the road and contentedly chewing their cuds. The car caravan was meandering along the dusty crowded streets of a small Indian village. The driver of the writer's car was moving rather carefully through a melange of people occupying the dusty road. The people were carrying all types and shapes of bundles and burdens. Children were everywhere with some of them throwing chunks of dried dirt about. A few hungry-looking dogs, their bodies bearing the weight of borderline starvation, skulked about. Some boys pedaled bicycles apparently not concerned with probable collisions with other objects in their paths. The driver, blowing the horn frequently, continued along his route and people seemed to get out of the way just before being struck by the car.

Snaking among the crowds, the car caravan seemed to be approaching the end of a rather precarious drive through all the humanity in that village. Suddenly it happened! Crash! The car brakes ground the car to a skidding halt. Loud voices were heard. The dust started to clear. By the left front car wheel lay a young boy. Clad in dirty clothes he lay face down in the dirt and remained motionless. The driver got out of the car. An old ragged man picked up the boy in his arms. As a crowd gathered, foreign-like words and cries of a native dialect were heard. Waving arms were visible and accusing fingers were pointed in the direction of the car caravan.

In a spirit of compassion, coupled with a desire to help out, the writer opened the car door and joined in the banter between the driver and the most vocal members of the milling crowd of people. The writer asked if his group could help by transporting the injured boy by car to a nearby hospital. The pleading question was answered by the driver who, in a commanding voice, said to get back into the car and not to become involved. The driver then engaged in an exchange of shouted challenges. Finally, displaying a clenched fist and making some closing remarks, the driver returned to the car, rolled up the windows, started the engine, gradually moved the car to the center of the road, and drove away.

Later on the driver, when asked why he refused the suggestion of helping the injured boy, explained that although he was observing the rules of the road, the angry crowd would probably blame a passenger for the incident as he was the one that caused the car to be there in the first place. So, for safety purposes, the driver ordered the writer back into the car. This is rather curious reasoning. It demonstrates that when visiting places where the inhabitants view episodes differently from what a person is used to, it is best to rely on the professionals who feel a sense of obligation for their ward's safety.

Try to become informed about the country you are visiting and remember that you are the foreigner there. The world and its people exhibit a variety of cultures. Respect for people and their culture is very necessary. To gain the greatest enjoyment from traveling, greet hosts with an open mind, heart, and extend the hand of friendship.

* * * * * * * * *

IMMEDIATELY START TO ANSWER THE FOLLOWING TEN COMPREHENSION QUESTIONS. CIRCLE THE *MOST* CORRECT ANSWER. TAKE A REASONABLE AMOUNT OF TIME TO ANSWER THE QUESTIONS. YOU SHOULDN'T LOOK BACK INTO THE STORY FOR ANSWERS.

* * * * * * * * *

COMPREHENSION TEST SIX

___ 1) The bulk of the traveling to foreign lands is done today by people who a) are well prepared, b) live in western-type societies, c) are seeking to relieve tension and boredom.

___ 2) Which of the following pair of items are the main reasons that most people travel for pleasure? a) to view scenic beauty and observe other cultures, b) to educate themselves and participate in the joys of travel, c) to participate in exotic activities and pursue a different lifestyle.

___ 3) The story seemed to point out that most of the problems that befell the young man visiting Europe could have been avoided if he had a) properly planned for the trip, b) enough money to solve the problems he faced, c) taken care to travel at a more desirable time of the year.

___ 4) Which of the following was not a way described to help learn about a trip that is being planned? a) talking with personal friends who have traveled, b) attending travel lectures given by professionals, c) enrolling in a college level travel course.

___ 5) Which one of the following would likely be the least considered as a part of the total experience of taking a trip? a) the journey itself, b) the anticipation of a journey, c) the necessary clothing, travel arrangements, money, and where to go.

___ 6) Upon arrival in a foreign country, one most important thing a person needs to have planned for is a) to arrive at a time of day that is very convenient, b) to have some currency of the country being visited, c) what to do if you are not allowed to enter the country.

___ 7) If the novice traveler is planning a solo trip to some remote place, probably the most important thing to do would be a) to secure a package tour, b) to make sure of food and lodging accommodations, c) to have considerable knowledge about the place being visited.

___ 8) The story brought out that, in addition to having a huge population, India also has one of the world's greatest concentrations of domestic a) monkeys, b) dogs, c) cattle.

___ 9) The incident with the injured boy, while traveling in India, pointed out how important it is to rely a) on one's basic instincts, b) on not becoming involved in situations, c) the professional advice of one who knows the culture.

___ 10) Mainly, this story is about a) how important planning is when taking a trip, b) how to visit exotic places, c) where to find out how to make a journey to a foreign country.

* * * * * * * * *

CHECK YOUR ANSWERS AGAINST THE KEY ON PAGE 103. CONVERT YOUR READING TIME TO RATE USING THE CHART ON PAGE 104. REMEMBER, ONCE YOU HAVE CONVERTED READING TIME INTO WORDS PER MINUTE (WPM) IT IS NO LONGER NECESSARY TO KEEP A RECORD OF THE READING TIME THAT IT TAKES YOU TO READ EACH STORY. CHART YOUR READING RATE (WPM) AND COMPREHENSION SCORE ON THE READING RATE GRAPH AND READING COMPREHENSION GRAPH ON PAGES 177 AND 178.

* * * * * * * * *

PRACTICE BEFORE THE NEXT LESSON

1) Remember that your goal is to read fast, effectively, and with comprehension. Don't become a slave to a reading rate. Keep your reading rate in a proper perspective. It will always be necessary to adjust your reading rate according to the type of materials being read.

2) Choose several kinds of materials on which to practice, such as technical reading, a novel, magazine, and newspapers. Preview each one, keep in mind your purposes for reading each one, apply appropriate skill goals, and vary your reading rate as necessary.

3) Read magazine or newspaper stories and look for a Setting, Characters, Action, Climax, and Conclusion. Mastery of this technique will assist you in previewing and help with speed and comprehension.

4) Remember that whatever you read while practicing you will be a) reading against time, b) toward a goal, or c) improving upon your past performance — or any combination of the three.

5) Choose many simple columnar materials on which to practice. Use a relaxed eye fix and force yourself to read down the page just as fast as you can force yourself to read.

6) So many good reading practices were introduced in Lesson Five you should review all 16 of them and then do some of the activities that were presented in the Practice Before the Next Lesson section.

* * * * * * * * * *

Answers — Comprehension Test Six — 1) b, 2) a, 3) a, 4) c, 5) b, 6) b, 7) a, 8) c, 9) c, 10) a

* * * * * * * * * *

Time	Rate—WPM	Time	Rate—WPM
1:00	1818	5:30	331
1:10	1558	5:40	321
1:20	1364	5:50	312
1:30	1212	6:00	303
1:40	1091	6:10	295
1:50	992	6:20	287
2:00	909	6:30	280
2:10	839	6:40	273
2:20	779	6:50	266
2:30	727	7:00	260
2:40	682	7:10	254
2:50	642	7:20	248
3:00	606	7:30	242
3:10	574	7:40	237
3:20	545	7:50	232
3:30	519	8:00	227
3:40	496	8:10	223
3:50	474	8:20	218
4:00	455	8:30	214
4:10	436	8:40	210
4:20	420	8:50	206
4:30	404	9:00	202
4:40	390	9:10	198
4:50	376	9:20	195
5:00	364	9:30	191
5:10	352	9:40	188
5:20	341	9:50	185
		10:00	182

Lesson Seven
REVIEW AND SKIMMING

In this lesson you will be introduced to skimming, which is a totally significant speed reading skill. In fact all those things you have done in the previous six lessons have allowed you to progress to the point of being able to skim, which speed reading students must do and of which they are generally frightened. So as to bolster your confidence to attack skimming as a speed reading technique, let's review all those skills that you have mastered so far which have paved the road to skimming and the subsequent benefits of really reading fast.

Lesson One — Here you committed yourself to doing the activities in this book that will help you to read fast. Statistical data were presented that proved students can read much faster, still retaining satisfactory comprehension. Other statistics showed that it wasn't necessary to be a genius to read fast and still have satisfactory comprehension.

Lesson Two — In this lesson you learned about the necessity of previewing — title, first paragraph, topic sentence of each paragraph, and last paragraph. Also you learned about the significance of the basic eye movements of the eye fix and the return sweep.

Lesson Three — It is important to maintain a positive attitude so that you can read faster with satisfactory comprehension. Here you were introduced to the poor reading habits that caused you to read slowly. These poor reading habits were: 1) Tracing with a finger, 2) Moving your head while reading, 3) Regressing, 4) Reading slowly, such as at an oral rate, and those related bad habits of lip movement, sounding words under the breath, and subvocalizing each word being read, and that most difficult problem to overcome, 5) Becoming hung-up on comprehension which is a fear that if you read fast you won't understand what you read. This simply is not true.

Lesson Four — The characteristics of speed reading were treated in this lesson: 1) The learning plateau on which students often find themselves and from which it can be difficult to move on to higher levels, 2) The necessity to unlearn bad habits, 3) An initial decrease in comprehension as you grapple with good speed reading techniques at the expense of old, poor reading habits, 4) That you become uncomfortable while struggling to rid yourself of bad reading habits and to establish good ones, and 5) A great deal of repetition and practice is necessary to learn to read fast.

To learn speed reading skills it is necessary to use simple materials. It is assumed that a student has an adequate vocabulary and the basic reading ability to learn to read fast. Use a relaxed eye fix on all materials that are being read.

Lesson Five — Here the importance of the retinal image in relation to comprehension and the somewhat mechanical process of speed reading were discussed. The following 16 good speed reading practices were presented: 1) Reduce the number of eye fixes, 2) Reduce the length of the return sweep, 3) Be relaxed and comfortable while practicing, 4) Practice your lessons in the same place if possible, 5) Be aware of performing the act of reading, 6) Practice to develop a skill, 7) Use simple reading materials, 8) Use a relaxed eye fix, 9) Practice to increase the eye span, 10) Read phrases of words, 11) Read down the column or page of words, 12) Use a finger or object to pace down the column of words or page, 13) Get rid of poor reading habits, 14) Use a skimming technique (covered later in this lesson), 15) Overcome the comprehension hang-up, and 16) Force yourself to read faster.

Lesson Six — Very high reading rates have been achieved with satisfactory comprehension. It is necessary to adjust your reading rate according to type of material being read, such as technical materials, novels, or textbooks.

To aid in previewing a story in order to read with greater speed and comprehension, it is necessary to recognize the parts of a story: 1) Setting, 2) Characters, 3) Action, 4) Climax, and 5) Conclusion.

While doing speed reading lessons you are always reading: 1) Against time, 2) Toward a goal, or 3) To improve on past performances; or any combination of the three.

You have just reviewed the speed reading techniques that were presented in the past six lessons. You have mastered those speed reading techniques by now and are ready to learn how to do that most important speed reading technique, skimming!

OPENING STATEMENT

All speed readers develop a certain reading style. There are some variations where readers use techniques that aren't taught but are adapted for their own personal use. A young student of mine made tremendous gains in his reading rate and always had 95 to 100 percent comprehension. When asked to describe his reading style, which also included the usual speed reading techniques, he stated that he would pick out nouns and verbs when reading. He didn't know how he had learned to do this and I had never heard of this reading method but for him it worked and I wasn't about to tamper with his success.

A rather standardized reading style includes reading all, or almost all, words in a very fast manner. You used this method while taking the Rate and Comprehension Test in Lesson Six. The other portion of this reading style includes skimming to which the remainder of the lesson is devoted. Speed readers tend to combine the aforementioned reading methods into a reading style that allows them alternately to skim and to slow down and read more slowly when it is necessary to do so.

To read with speed you must skim. Yet readers are reluctant to practice and master skimming because they are afraid they will not comprehend what they read. To help you to understand the technique of skimming, use a telephone book and look for the name of a friend. Read down the column of names. You rapidly pass over unfamiliar names but see how the name of your friend stands out! A lawyer student of mine stated that learning to skim helped him, when researching past legal actions to determine those cases that applied to his current case, to quickly discard those cases that didn't apply.

Read simple materials and set your mind to the task of mastering the skimming technique. Remember that without skimming the human eye can, when viewing every word, see only about 800 words per minute. This is the absolute upper limit and you will be uncomfortable trying to read with speed using only this method.

SKILLS AND TECHNIQUES —
SKIMMING!

Choose some simple materials to read and practice on them in the following sequence in order to develop the ability to skim:

1) Read the first paragraph of the story as this often gives you the setting of the story,

2) Read both the first and last sentences of all the other paragraphs. Remember that a paragraph expresses one idea and all the sentences in the paragraph support that one idea. If the paragraph is especially a long one also read a sentence from the middle. Quite often the main idea is expressed in the first of last sentence of a paragraph and the main idea of a paragraph is what you really want to remember.

3) Read the last paragraph of the story as it often presents the conclusion of the story just read. Before you say that this will give the plot of a story away, remember that you are gaining the skill of skimming and that is the most important thing. Unless you are reading a suspenseful novel, knowing the total plot of the story is what you want to comprehend. Once you master the skimming technique of reading you can read printed matter at whatever rates that best suit you.

4) Titles, subtitles, pictures, etc., in a story should be included in the skimming process as you read through the printed material.

Keep in mind that you are practicing the skimming technique and will master the skill if you use simple materials and concentrate on the skimming process. Force yourself to skim! You will experience the usual problems associated with learning to skim such as trying to locate where the last sentence of a paragraph begins and the mechanics of looking only for first sentences and main thoughts of paragraphs. This is to be expected. Mastering the skimming technique will take considerable time and effort. Practice the skimming sequence presented in this Skills and Techniques section again and again. Don't become discouraged with skimming as it is absolutely essential to speed reading.

When skimming while reading you tend to be overly conscious of seeing every word. Suffice it to say that it isn't necessary to read each word to have satisfactory comprehension. However, to quiet your fears about not understanding what you read because you don't see every word, recall the retinal image that was discussed in Lesson Five. As you read, many words which you are not consciously aware of seeing appear on the retina of the eye and your brain "sees" the words. Therefore you see and comprehend words and meanings in this way in addition to those words you consciously see.

GOAL SETTING

Your goal will be to begin the mastery of the skimming technique which will take you some time to attain.

1) Use the sequence of skimming methods that was presented in the Skills and Techniques section of this lesson. Practice until you become more comfortable with the sequential technique.

2) Always have a goal in mind in either words per minute (WPM) or time when you do your Rate and Comprehension Test. You used these two goal setting methods in Lessons 5 and 6. Which one of the two seem to have produced the best results for you? Informal polling of my speed reading

students indicates about a 50-50 split in using either WPM or time. Use whichever one that best fits your reading style. You might still want to experiment with both when doing other Rate and Comprehension Tests in later lessons. To assist you in setting a WPM or time goal, refer to the results you have achieved on past stories that are recorded on the Reading Rate Graph on page 177.

3) In Lesson Six your goal was to read the Rate and Comprehension Test Story down the page as fast as you could, reading all or almost all the words. In this lesson you are to skim by reading the first paragraph, the first and last sentence of each paragraph, and the last paragraph. Stay with the skimming method throughout the entire story.

4) Warm-up on a Rate and Comprehension Test story previously read and force yourself to read fast.

* * * * * * * * *

RATE AND COMPREHENSION TEST

Read the following story, "Some Useful Native Plants of the West." Be sure to refer to the procedure for taking this test that was described under the Skills and Techniques section of Lesson One. Do this right now. *Do the following for this and each of the ten Rate and Comprehension Tests in this book.*

1) Read the story,

2) Keep track of the time taken to read the story in minutes and seconds and *write it down,*

3) Take the comprehension test,

4) Use the chart at the end of the lesson to figure your reading rate (WPM),

5) Use the answer key at the end of the lesson to figure your comprehension level,

6) Chart your scores on the Reading Rate and Comprehension Graphs on pages 177 and 178,

7) You will need a watch, or some type of timepiece, on which to keep track of the time it takes you to read the test story,

8) Think of the speed reading goals presented in the Goal Setting portion of this lesson before you begin to read the test story.

* * * * * * * * * *

* * Set your timepiece — read the story * *

SOME USEFUL NATIVE PLANTS OF THE WEST

by Jeanette Coyle

Have you ever strolled in an open field, a shaded forest, a flat, gravelly desert, or explored a scrubby hillside and wondered to yourself which plants there are edible or useful to man? In today's modern and hectic pace, people are escaping more to nature for quiet moments of solitude and relaxation. This need to return to nature has kindled a renewed interest for many to learn the secrets of native plants as sources of food, medicine, and a variety of other uses.

Many of the methods of collecting and preparing native plant materials for consumption and use were well known by California Indians and early Spanish settlers as a matter of course for survival long before the present residents arrived. Today's modern hiker, camper, or naturalist often appreciates these skills only as an interesting hobby, but the skills are just as true and useful today as they were many years ago. A few of the more common and interesting useful native plants are discussed here.

In California a hiker in the chaparral-covered foothills may come across a six-to-ten-foot-tall evergreen shrub called "Toyon" or "Christmas Berry" (*Heteromeles arbutifolia*). It has narrow serrated leaves and displays small white flowers in terminal clusters in the summer, ripening into small red berries in time for Christmas. Native birds were the first residents to eat the tart fruit, but native Indians, followed by Mexicans, and then American settlers, soon learned to prize the berry as a source of food. The berries were ground into a meal after being baked in earthen ovens for two to three days. The fruit could also be roasted in parching baskets as they were tossed with coals and heated stones. The slight cooking took away the bitter taste that makes the fresh fruit rarely eaten.

A shrub that many people recognized by its twisting red branches which finds itself cut and polished and displayed in many gift shops is the "Manzanita" (*Arctostaphylos*). Berries of almost 43 species of "Manzanita" were gathered green by the Spanish settlers and made into jelly or a soft drink. The Indians gathered only the ripe berries and ground them into a meal. Several Indian tribes celebrated the "Manzanita" harvest with feasting and dancing. Berries at this time were eaten fresh, but large quantities were dried and stored for winter use. The meal of the dried and crushed seeds was made into a mush and shaped into a flat cake that was baked in hot ashes. The leaves of "Manzanita" was applied to soothe the irritated skin. it seems this habit formed only after the onslaught of white settlers. If a rash from poison oak developed, a lotion made from the leaves of the "Manzanita" was applied to sooth the irritated skin.

One of the most widely used native plants by western Indians was "Chia" (*Salvia columbariae*). This blue-flowered sage is a small herbaceous plant ranging in height from five to twenty-five inches. Found commonly in the desert, chaparral, or grassy sage areas, the small grayish seeds were easily dislodged by careful beating of the heads over a large flat basket. After being ground into a meal, a mucilagenous sticky mass resulted when hot water was added. A nut-like flavor characterized the "Chia" seed flour when baked into biscuits or cakes. The seeds of "Chia" are reputed to have nourished Indians on a full day's march across hot dry land. Stories are related of Indian braves running from Yuma, Arizona, to San Diego, California, on a few teaspoonsful of "Chia" seeds and a small amount of water in a kind of early day "pony express" system. A teaspoon of "Chia" seeds in a quart of water from a brackish desert water hole is reputed to neutralize the bad water and make a nourishing and thirst quenching drink.

Leaves of the "Chia" were chewed as a cure for colds and smoked and steamed in sweathouses. Crushed leaves were mixed with water for use as dye, shampoo and hair straightener. Fresh leaves were crushed into a poultice and placed in the armpits at bedtime to rid the body of odors, a necessary precaution for men going on hunt, so game could not ferret out the human scent. One seed could be placed in the eye and rolled around to amazingly clean the eye. "Chia" was a very important staple food of the Pacific Coast Indians as proved by the large quantities of seeds found in archeological digs of the buried dead. "Chia" is cultivated today and sold in health food stores for its highly nutritive and energy-giving properties. If collected in the wild, the harvest time is from June to September.

Bulbous plants, mostly from the lily family, were used extensively by California Indians. Species of *(Brodiaea)*, "Indian Onion," and *(Allium)*, the "Wild Onion," were used for seasoning or eaten roasted, boiled, creamed, stewed, or in soups. The "Mariposa Lily" *(Calochortus)* was dug up from open woods and valleys and was eaten raw or roasted up to twenty-four hours until brown and soft in earth ovens lined with stones. "Mariposa Lily" species usually display solitary, showy flowers ranging in color from pale yellow to scarlet and white to deep lavender. The bulb of the blue-flowered "Camus" (*Camanssia quamash)* was rendered into a soft sweet mass by steaming in a pit fire for at least twenty-four hours. The substance was either eaten fresh or dried into a cake and stored to meet future needs. "Camus" is commonly found in moist meadows of forested mountains.

Desert plants commonly used by early residents included the "Mescal" or "Century Plant" *(Agave)*. The familiar towering stalk may grow from seven to nine feet from a rosette of thick succulent leaves. These flower stalks were plucked from the plant just before the flowers opened, then baked through the night between the leaves, in covered pit ovens. The juicy sweet flower heads were eaten immediately or formed into cakes and stored for the future. These dried cakes were also used as the base of a sweet drink when boiled with water. If allowed to form before cutting, the *Agave* seeds were collected and ground into flour for use as gruel. However, the principal food source of *Agave* was the base. The leaves were removed and the basal crown was roasted in a hole. When tender, it tasted like coarse, juicy, not-so-sweet potatoes. The abundance of this desert plant made it a staple native food. South of the border, species of "Century Plant" mash is fermented and distilled into Tequila and Mescal. The charcoal from burned *Agave* was used for tattooing. Fibers from the pulverized leaves were made into rope. Unforfunately, any use of this plant meant its complete destruction.

Found in desert, chaparral, and juniper-piñon woodlands is the *Yucca*, ranging from small shrubs to fairly large trees such as the "Joshua Tree." The creamy flowers, purple-tinged buds, and young flowering stalks were eaten raw in the field or added to a salad. The numerous dagger-like yellow-green leaves supplied the Indian with fibers for sandals, cords, baskets, and rough cloth. During World War I, millions of pounds of burlap material was made from *Yucca*. The roots produced a lather when cut, mashed, and rubbed vigorously in water. A laxative also was derived from the roots. The seeds and fresh fruit were eaten too. If the flower stalk was cut before the flowers opened, they were prepared by roasting or boiling and removing the tough outer layers.

The present trend in ecological and survival arts has created a renewed interest in aboriginal uses of native plants. Present California residents are most fortunate to have such an unparalleled abundance of native plants that are still available for the modern-day homemaker, hiker, and gastronomic adventurer.

* * * * * * * * * *

* * * * * * * * * *

COMPREHENSION TEST SEVEN

___ 1) Study about the use of native plants as sources of food, medicine, etc., by Indians and early settlers is currently pursued by people as a) a hobby, b) for survival purposes, c) a method of supplementing the food used for household meals.

___ 2) The fresh fruit of the "Toyon" was rarely eaten because a) the only way the fruit was made edible was through cooking, b) the fruit was too tart unless properly prepared, c) of the bitter taste.

___ 3) For which of the following did the Indians probably not use the "Manzanita"? a) fresh fruit, b) a lotion for poison oak, c) smoking tobacco.

___ 4) "Chia," a blue-flowered plant ranging in height from five to twenty-five inches, is a member of what plant family? a) *Agave*, b) sage, c) onion.

___ 5) "Chia" leaves were made into a poultice and used to rid the body of odors a) for vanity purposes, b) to cleanse the pores of the skin, c) so the scent of man wouldn't frighten game.

___ 6) The *Agave* was used for everything from food to tattooing but unfortunately a) any use of the plant meant its complete destruction, b) the plant has always been in short supply, c) attempts to domestically cultivate the plant have been unsuccessful.

___ 7) The largest member of the *Yucca* plant family is the a) "Century Plant," b) "Joshua Tree," c) "Chaparral."

___ 8) A conclusion can be drawn that the abundance of useful native plants available to California Indians a) kept them well fed and clothed, b) provided an opportunity to commercially use the plants in more recent times, c) contributed to a hunting and gathering existence.

___ 9) According to the many uses of "Chia," eating the seeds of this plant would probably benefit what group of modern-day people? a) athletes, b) health-food devotees, c) people who are ill.

___ 10) Mainly this story is about plants and a) how they may be used, b) their aboriginal uses, c) how they can be used in a survival situation.

* * * * * * * * * *

CHECK YOUR ANSWERS AGAINST THE KEY ON PAGE 119. CONVERT YOUR READING TIME TO RATE USING THE CHART ON PAGE 120. REMEMBER, ONCE YOU HAVE CONVERTED READING TIME INTO WORDS PER MINUTE (WPM) IT IS NO LONGER NECESSARY TO KEEP A RECORD OF THE READING TIME IT TAKES YOU TO READ EACH STORY. CHART YOUR READING RATE (WPM) AND COMPREHENSION SCORE ON

THE READING RATE GRAPH AND READING COMPREHENSION
GRAPH ON PAGES 177 AND 178.

* * * * * * * * * *

PRACTICE BEFORE THE NEXT LESSON

The following activities will help you to practice
and master the technique of skimming:

1) Use the telephone book as was suggested in
the Opening Statement of this lesson. Look up the
names of your friends as you pace your eyes down
the column of telephone subscribers.

2) Choose some short stories to read and use the
process of reading the first paragraph, the first and
last sentence of each paragraph, and the last
paragraph as was suggested in the Skills and
Techniques portion of this lesson. To help you
practice this technique, pencil in a bracket in the
margin beside the first and last paragraphs of the
story. Underline the first and last sentences of each
paragraph. This will help call your attention to the
parts of the story that are necessary to recognize in
order to learn how to skim. Then skim through the
story paying attention to the areas you have
marked. Stories in newspapers or magazines would
be fine sources of material on which to practice in
the aforementioned manner.

* * * * * * * * * *

Answers — Comprehension Test Seven — 1) a,
2) c, 3) c, 4) b, 5) c, 6) a, 7) b, 8) c, 9) a,
10 b

* * * * * * * * * *

Time	Rate—WPM	Time	Rate—WPM
1:00	1298	5:00	260
1:10	1113	5:10	251
1:20	974	5:20	243
1:30	865	5:30	236
1:40	779	5:40	229
1:50	708	5:50	223
2:00	649	6:00	216
2:10	599	6:10	210
2:20	556	6:20	205
2:30	519	6:30	200
2:40	487	6:40	195
2:50	458	6:50	190
3:00	433	7:00	185
3:10	410	7:10	181
3:20	389	7:20	177
3:30	371	7:30	173
3:40	354	7:40	169
3:50	339	7:50	166
4:00	324	8:00	162
4:10	312	8:10	159
4:20	300	8:20	156
4:30	288	8:30	153
4:40	278	8:40	150
4:50	269		

Lesson Eight
VOCABULARY AND
COMPREHENSION

It is presumed that students motivated to become speed readers possess the necessary reading ability, including an adequate *vocabulary*, to develop speed reading skills. For this reason, vocabulary and word recognition skills have not been emphasized. Students have inquired if, when practicing their speed reading materials, they should stop when they come to a word they don't recognize and turn to a dictionary to find its meaning. My answer is *not to stop!* Whenever a student is practicing to develop speed reading skills, he should move ahead in whatever he is reading and not regress. To learn a speed reading skill, which would be the goal, is more important than the word meaning. However, a review of some basic word recognition methods seem to be in order.

Phonics and context clues are two common word recognition methods that can be used to help you with your vocabulary. Let's begin with phonics. Every letter of the alphabet is either a vowel or consonant. Letter sounds, letter blends, and syllables (which are parts of words) can help you to analyze words phonetically.

Vowels — Every word in our language contains at least one vowel. Vowels often have a long sound (as in ate) or a short sound (as in at). Generally, if a word has a single vowel the sound is short (as in bit) and if a word ends in a silent "e" (as in bite) the vowel sound is long. If a word contains two vowels together (as in coat), frequently the first vowel is long and the second one is silent.

Consonants are the rest of the letters of the alphabet and are usually separated in words or syllables by vowels (as in bit). Two or three consonants together which develop their own sounds are called blends. An example of a two-letter consonant blend would be the "bl" in blend. An example of a three-letter consonant blend would the the "str" in strong. The consonant "R" has a very strong sound and tends to dominate other nearby letter sounds.

Syllables are parts of words and must contain at least one vowel. The two most common principles about syllables are:

1) When a vowel is followed by two consonants and then another vowel (VC/CV) the syllable break is between the two consonants.

2) When a vowel is followed by a single consonant and then a vowel (V/CV) the syllable break is between the first vowel and consonant.

A *prefix* is a syllable added to the beginning of a word to modify its meaning as the "pre" in preheat. A *suffix* is a syllable added to the end of a word to modify its meaning as the "ed" in preheated.

Synonyms are words with similar meanings such as solitary and alone. *Antonyms* are words with opposite meanings such as melancholy and joy. *Homonyms* are words that are similar in sound such as their and there.

Another method of word recognition is to use the most common of all reading skills, the *context clue*. The other words in the context of a story give you clues to both pronunciation and/or the meaning of a word. See how the other words in the context gives clues to the meaning of the word "edifice" in the following sentence: "The new high-rise building, a twenty story edifice, contains a bank on the ground level, a restaurant on the top floor, and office space on the other floors."

To aid in the development of vocabulary you can utilize the following:

1) Keep a dictionary close by, to which you can readily refer, in the area where you customarily practice your speed reading.

2) Maintain a word list of those words you encounter that you didn't recognize or want to make a part of your reading vocabulary. Remember to make a word list after you have finished practicing your speed reading skills.

3) Set a goal to learn a certain number of words each week.

4) Read a great deal as the exposure to that many more words will help to increase vocabulary.

5) Practice using the word recognition methods presented in the beginning of this lesson.

OPENING STATEMENT

In past lessons you have studied aspects of comprehension particularly when doing Rate and Comprehension Tests. In order to gain the broadest viewpoint regarding comprehension about anything that you read, the following thoughts are presented:

1) Comprehension is the ultimate goal in reading.

2) Preview most of the material you read, especially any that you must remember.

3) Before you begin to read, ask yourself what you want to learn from the story and what message you think the author will be trying to get across. To test out this idea choose a newspaper story and apply the question after reading the headline and the first paragraph. When you determine what you

feel the idea is that the writer is trying to get across, preview the story, read the story, and measure the results against your initial thoughts. Eventually you can gain clues as to the context of a story through titles, headlines, and previewing.

4) There are two basic kinds of thought processes in comprehension, literal and inferential. Literal is remembering words and meanings exactly as they are expressed in a story. For example a story might state, "It was a sunny day at the beach." If given a choice to answer what kind of a day it was at the beach — sunny, cloudy, rainy — the answer would be sunny because this was directly stated in the story. Inferential means to infer meaning through reasoning because the thought isn't exactly spelled out in the context of the story. By putting several thoughts together you can determine meanings. For example a story might state, "The boy ran onto the beach and the hot sand burned the bottom of his feet." If given a choice to answer what kind of a day it was at the beach — sunny, cloudy, rainy — the answer would be to infer that it was sunny because the hot sand had burned the bottom of the boy's feet. Inferential comprehension requires a higher thought process than literal and authors frequently use it in fictional stories to allow the reader to fill in details and arrive at conclusions upon his own. This involves the reader in the story and makes for more interesting reading.

5) If you are a student, a pleasure reader, a doctor, or whatever, you will assess the level of difficulty of the material that you intend to read and just how important the material appears to you. At this point you may determine if you will merely read the material or if it is important to

preview, skim, read, and even possibly re-read if necessary.

6) Locating the topic sentence which contains the thought of a paragraph can save the reader a great amount of time. A paragraph expresses a single thought. All other sentences in the paragraph support that thought expressed in the topic sentence. Look for the topic sentence to occur most often at the beginning of the paragraph, next most often at the end of the paragraph, and lastly in the interior of the paragraph. Look for topic sentences because the thoughts they express make up the story plot.

SKILLS AND TECHNIQUES

There might be occasions when you will want to prepare a story, other than one from this book, to read for rate (WPM). Since you will not possess the basic ingredients beforehand that are necessary to determine WPM, whenever you come across a story that you would like to read for rate purposes, follow this general procedure:

1) Preview the story as you have done whenever taking any of the previous seven Rate and Comprehension stories.

2) Read the story, using all the speed reading skills that you possess, for rate and keep track of the time it takes you to read the story (in minutes and portions of minutes).

Now to the mechanics of how to figure your reading rate in this situation:

1) After reading the story, measure four inches of lines of words (vertically — down the page).

2) Count every word in the four inches of print and divide this total by four. This will give the average number of words per inch.

3) Measure the total number of inches in print (all the pages) in the entire story and multiply this total by the average number of words per inch. You might not want to choose too long a story over which to test your reading rate. This action will give you an approximation of the total number of words in the entire story and is accurate enough to determine your reading rate.

4) Divide the number of minutes that it took you to read the story (express any fractions of minutes as decimals, i.e., two and one-half minutes as 2.5) into the total number of words in the story. This will give you your reading rate. All this appears complicated. Expressed as a formula it appears thusly: Number of words in the story $\div$ time (minutes) = WPM.

GOAL SETTING

1) Warm-up on some stories that you have already read. Use the relaxed eye fix; read down the column or page of words; pick out some topic sentences from the paragraphs; and force yourself to read just as fast as you can.

2) To assist in comprehension, on the Rate and Comprehension Test story, ask yourself what you want to learn from the story and what you think the author will be trying to get across. When you get to the Rate and Comprehension Test story, apply these two items after you have read the title and first paragraph of the story.

3) Comprehension questions are either literal (answers are directly stated in the story) or inferential (add up several ideas stated in the story to arrive at the answer). After you have answered the 10 comprehension questions and are checking your answers, you will find, identified, which questions are literal and which are inferential.

4) When reading the Rate and Comprehension Test story, be sure to look for topic sentences, most often the first sentence of a paragraph, as you read rapidly through the story.

5) Establish a goal to read the Rate and Comprehension Test story the fastest that you have ever read. Set a goal in either words per minute (WPM) or time.

6) During Lessons Six and Seven you either read all the words as fast as you possibly could, or almost all the words in the story; or skimmed. Most readers combine the two styles. You can compare the rate and comprehension results by consulting your progress graphs on pages 177 and 178. With the Rate and Comprehension Test story you might want either to skim, read most of the words as fast as you can, or use a combination of the two. Employ an experimental attitude as you choose your reading method. You want to increase your rate and *not* be overly concerned about comprehension!

* * * * * * * * * *

RATE AND COMPREHENSION TEST

Read the following story, "Family Car: A Vehicle for Liberation." Be sure to refer to the procedure for taking this test that was described under the Skills and Techniques section of Lesson One. Do this right now. *Do the following for this and each of the ten Rate and Comprehension Tests in this book.*

1) Read the story,

2) Keep track of the time taken to read the story in minutes and seconds and *write it down,*

3) Take the comprehension test,

4) Use the chart at the end of the lesson to figure your reading rate (WPM),

5) Use the answer key at the end of the lesson to figure your comprehension level,

6) Chart your scores on the Reading Rate and Comprehension Graphs of pages 177 and 178,

7) You will need a watch, or some type of timepiece, on which to keep track of the time it takes you to read the test story,

8) Think of the speed reading goals presented in the Goal Setting portion of this lesson before you begin to read the test story.

* * * * * * * * * *

* * Set your timepiece — read the story * *

FAMILY CAR: A VEHICLE FOR LIBERATION
by Ralph Margolis

Surely this was a recipe for pleasure. Take a comfortable family car; in it place two teenagers and two adults who are related to each other and are on friendly terms; then set this against the background of a balmy spring day. Have them starting out for a little ride just to enjoy themselves It should have been pleasant but unfortunately another ingredient, unexpected and unwanted, fell into the recipe and therein lies the story.

"Hey, Dad," observed Zach, who was driving, "That's a pretty bad miss."

The father glanced up and down the street but saw nothing extraordinary. "Sorry, Son," he exclaimed with a little laugh, "But I can't see any kind of miss."

The mother's eyes had also darted about and with as much success. "Whatever are you talking about, Zach?" she wondered aloud.

"I can tell you, Mom," volunteered Mimi, the sister. "Can you feel how the car sort of bucks and jerks? That's called missing. The engine's power should come in a smooth steady flow. Some of the power impulses are missing so the car jerks. The common expression is that we have got a pretty bad miss."

Mother sighed. She didn't know whether to be relieved or nervous. Dad, on the other hand, ha-ha'd a little because he had understood the symptoms and had tried to make a little joke out of it. Clearly, no one else had seen the humor in it.

"Fine," said Mother to Father. "So what are you going to do about it, Ralph?"

"The usual, Melba," Ralph replied with considerable assurance. "The car is due for a tune-up but the miss will go away by itself when the engine warms up."

"Tune-up? Warm-up?" echoed Melba.

"Oh sure," said Mimi. "We learned all about it in school. Tune-up is checking the spark plugs and things to make sure the engine runs right. Sort of like checking the tubes in a TV."

"And warm-up," added Zach, "is to let the engine get up to normal operating temperature."

"And what is that?" asked Mother.

"Around 160^0," replied Mimi.

"Around 200^0," stated Zach.

Melba was proud of both children and she didn't want to show any favoritism for either answer over the other, so she responded with a motherly, "My how smart you both are." Ralph understood his wife's position so he quickly explained that both answers were right. Normal operation temperature was a range of numbers, not a particular number. Moreover, 160°-200° was a good spread and occupied the middle of the heat gauge. This, however, seemed to Melba to be excessively hot and she expressed herself to that effect.

Now it was Zach's turn to explain. "Look at it this way," he rejoined. "The engine is metal and oil. If it was a frying pan you couldn't cook an egg very fast at that temperature."

"If it *were* . . . " Melba corrected his grammar. Here she was on firmer ground. The truth was that Melba experienced just a twinge of frustration. It began to look as if this pleasure ride was turning into a lesson in, of all things, auto-mechanics whereas her intentions had been to see the spring flowers and shrubs and even pick up some ideas on landscaping. Besides, all this knowledge exhibited by her family was balanced against her own ignorance of things mechanical. Outloud she postulated, "Well, if the car needs fixing, let's get it fixed."

The car smoothened out; it just purred along. "See," stated Father, "the car is warmed up and the miss is gone. It's been acting this way for a few days." He was pleased with the accuracy of his forecast but promised to take the car to a garage soon. His confident smile faded, however, as the car began to shake again.

"Uh, oh," said Zach, cold apprehension in his

voice. "She's doing it again."

Mimi agreed, "And it's worse this time."

"Hey Son," suggested Ralph, "Better bring it in for a landing. Good thing this is a quiet street with lots of parking."

The engine went dead. It stopped completely but Zach was able to coast the car to the curb. Pushing was not necessary. This turn of events was so dramatic and unexpected that Zach just sat gripping the steering wheel as if stunned. Ralph, who could usually be counted on to make light conversation when the going was good, sat speechless and momentarily bewildered. Mimi looked shocked and could say only, "Oh dear, oh dear, oh dear, what are we going to do?"

A few seconds dragged by. Then Melba, with the optimism born of complete faith in her family, brightened. "Let's try to fix it ourselves. If we can't, then we'll call a garage to come and get us."

The four of them climbed out of the car, raised the hood and surveyed the fresh carcass of their dead engine. Its proud glory was a thing of the recent past much like a warrior hero newly fallen on a battlefield. As each one examined the mortal remains, each perceived a different aspect. One saw mostly the accumulated stains, oil, and gritty grime. Another saw the welter of wires and hoses. Zach was impressed with the bulky air cleaner, alternator, distributor, and other surface accessories without which the machine is incomplete. And there, beneath all those ornaments, lay the massive engine block resting in peace at long last.

Melba was the only one not lost in thought or hypnotized or whatever, and maybe the only one doing some useful thinking. "Maybe," she asked, "maybe we're out of gas?"

"That's a good possibility. The symptoms fit," Ralph answered. "The engine missed badly, then went dead."

"We are not out of gas," stated Zach pointedly. "I filled the tank yesterday and we haven't exactly gone anywhere since."

"How about the spark plugs, Daddy?" asked Mimi.

Ralph thought about that for a moment, then said, "There could be one or two bad ones, but it isn't likely that all would go bad at exactly the same time and kill the engine. You know, just like TV tubes."

"No," he continued, "We must look for a single thing that would affect the whole engine's performance and give us all of the symptoms." While Ralph was speaking he haphazardly wiggled some things and tugged on others. Then, turning to his son, he commanded, "Zach, hit the starter. Maybe it will start now."

Zach ran the starter for a couple of seconds. It sounded normal but the engine did not catch.

"Dad?" Now it was his son's turn to make a suggestion. "Maybe it is something in the distributor. Check the breaker points and the condenser lead."

"Good idea, Son." Ralph found a screwdriver in the box of miscellany in the trunk and used it to snap off two spring clips at the sides of the distributor. Now the distributor cap with the circle of fat spark plug wires could be removed to one side. Ralph examined the uncovered parts carefully, then replaced the cap and clamped it down with the spring clips. The others could only guess what he was doing since his arched back was all they could see. "Nooooo," he confessed slowly, in the manner of one who is unsure. "Everything in the distributor looks normal. Not good, but really not very bad either. I'm stumped. Anybody got any good ideas?"

None were forthcoming. It seemed like a dismal way to end a little jaunt on a sunny day. Still, these things do happen. Mimi finally gave voice to the inevitable next step. "Well," she said, "better call a garage."

"OK," agreed Ralph. "I'll go."

"While you are doing that, is it all right if I wipe the goo off this wire with a tissue?" asked Melba. "It fell into the oil and really looks ugly."

"What wire?" asked Ralph, turning on his heel. His disappointment turned into curiosity at this new development. Melba showed him a slim dark wire, one end of which was not fastened to anything. It had dropped off of something and was stuck in an oily accumulation on top of the engine block. It would be very easy to overlook this because of the tangle of wires and low level of illumination under the car hood. One quick look and Ralph knew exactly where this wire should go.

"Hey, hey, hey," said he excitedly. "Eureka, you have found it. This is what caused all our trouble, Melba. You wonderful wife, you; you found it."

"How could that cause our troubles, Ralph?" asked Melba, pleased that she could be of use around a car after all.

"I'll tell you what this wire does for a living; then you'll understand its importance. It carries electricity from the ignition switch to the coil where the voltage is increased enough to make a spark at the spark plug. The wire somehow loosened and dropped off. When it was loose, the engine missed. When it fell off, the engine died."

Zach was looking too. "I'll bet," he surmised, "the little nut is in there too, somewhere."

Melba was still there and she asked in a voice which now betrayed considerable interest, "Would that really fix it?"

"Oh, Mom," cried Zach with adoration showing as he echoed her words. "Would that really fix it? It is fixed already." As an afterthought he added, "I'll bet you know a lot more about cars than you let on."

While Melba did not agree with him, she did not feel it necessary to debate the point with him. Meanwhile, Ralph had found the missing nut, wiped it and the wire clean, and replaced them properly with a small lock washer and wrench found in the miscellany box. The whole job was buttoned up in a matter of seconds. Next, Zach obeyed the order to start her up. It caught almost immediately, coughed a couple of times, then settled down to a most contented purr. The magnificent fighting body had been down but not out. The fallen hero had risen from the battlefield as if by a miracle. Indeed, this is how an engine will respond when important little wires are reconnected.

A few seconds later, they were back in the car and on their way. Mimi, Zach, and Ralph took turns detailing how Melba had saved the day. The truth was she enjoyed their praise and basked in the warm glow of it. Thoughts ran through her mind. Perhaps cars were interesting after all. Maybe a class in simple auto mechanics would be fun. Such classes are offered in adult evening school. As she fantasized, a little smile played across her lips. A good running car helps free a person.

IMMEDIATELY START TO ANSWER THE FOLLOWING TEN
COMPREHENSION QUESTIONS. CIRCLE THE *MOST*
CORRECT ANSWER. TAKE A REASONABLE AMOUNT OF
TIME TO ANSWER THE QUESTIONS. YOU SHOULDN'T LOOK
BACK INTO THE STORY FOR ANSWERS.

COMPREHENSION TEST EIGHT

___ 1) When the engine of a car causes a bucking
or jerking motion it could be that the
engine is a) coughing, b) back-firing,
c) missing.

___ 2) If the engine in the car had had a recent
professional tune-up probably the engine
would a) have run properly after the
engine warmed up, b) have run smoothly,
c) always start quickly.

___ 3) The proper operating temperature for an
automobile engine is probably a) 160°,
b) 180°, c) 200°.

___ 4) The person in the family who knows the
least about automobiles is a) Melba,
b) Mimi, c) Zach.

___ 5) The family member who was driving the
car when the engine went dead was
a) Ralph, b) Melba, c) Zach.

___ 6) After the engine stopped and members of
the family looked at the engine, Zach was
most impressed with a) stains, oil, and
grime, b) the bulky air cleaner, alternator,
distributor, and surface accessories,
c) the welter of wires and hoses.

___ 7) Which of the following was not a possibility, considered by the family, to have
caused the engine to stop? a) the
weather, b) fuel system, c) electrical system.

___ 8) It was suggested that the spark plugs in the engine weren't the problem because they, like TV tubes, would not a) be properly tightened, b) fail all at once, c) be fouled by carbon deposits.

___ 9) The one thing that caused the engine of the car to stop dead was a) a loose wire, b) a faulty ignition switch, c) a broken fuel pump.

___ 10) Mainly this story is about a) a family with a problem, b) the mother who saved the problem with the car, c) a balky car engine.

* * * * * * * * *

CHECK YOUR ANSWERS AGAINST THE KEY ON PAGE 138. CONVERT YOUR READING TIME TO RATE USING THE CHART ON PAGE 139. REMEMBER ONCE YOU HAVE CONVERTED READING TIME INTO WORDS PER MINUTE (WPM) IT IS NO LONGER NECESSARY TO KEEP A RECORD OF THE READING TIME THAT IT TAKES YOU TO READ EACH STORY. CHART YOUR READING RATE (WPM) AND COMPREHENSION SCORE ON THE READING RATE GRAPH AND READING COMPREHENSION GRAPH ON PAGES 177 AND 178.

PRACTICE BEFORE THE NEXT LESSON

1) In that place where you customarily do your speed reading lessons, to help you build vocabulary, keep a dictionary close by; maintain a list of words you didn't recognize the meaning of; and set a goal to learn a certain number of words per week.

2) To assist you in comprehension, choose a number of short stories (as in a newspaper), read the headline, the first paragraph, and then ask yourself what you want to learn from the story and what you think the author is trying to get across.

Then preview the story in the prescribed manner, read the story, and then measure the meaning you obtained against your initial analysis.

3) To help you determine just how important it is to you to understand the contents of a story, choose a reasonably long newspaper story and perform each of the following steps, pausing after each one to reflect on your comprehension: a) Preview (how much do you remember about the story?); b) Read the story using your speed reading style (how much do you remember about the story now?); and c) Re-read the story (how much do you remember about the story now?). Reflecting upon your comprehension of the story after each of the three steps will give you an idea of how you will need to read to gain the comprehension that you deem necessary.

4) Practice finding the topic sentences of paragraphs by consciously looking for first and last sentences of paragraphs as you read a newspaper or magazine story. Try not to read every word of the story and when you have finished, reflect upon what you have read and how much you comprehend about the message of the story. Looking for first and last sentences will cause you some difficulty until it becomes second nature and you truly can skim through reading materials using this method.

5) Choose a short newspaper or magazine story and use it to help you set up a story to check out your reading rate. Refer to the method to follow that is presented in the Skills and Techniques section of this lesson. Learning this skill will help you to check your reading rate whenever you desire to do so. The formula is: Number of words in the story ÷ time = WPM.

6) After you have practiced all these activities while reading the stories you have chosen, think about the two basic methods of a) reading all the words of a story as rapidly as you can force yourself to do so, or b) skimming. Is one or the other most comfortable to use? Are you combining the two methods as you read? Continue to use both methods as you read; don't stick to just one of them at this point, and be sure to maintain an experimental attitude as you continue to use the two methods.

7) Keep a current newspaper in that place where you regularly practice your speed reading skills. There will be many times that you will need to refer to it to practice specific skills.

* * * * * * * * * *

Answers — Comprehension Test Eight — 1) c, 2) b, 3) b, 4) a, 5) c, 6) b, 7) a, 8) b, 9 a, 10) a.
Literal questions — 1, 5, 6, 7, 8, and 9
Inferential questions — 2, 3, 4, and 10

* * * * * * * * * *

Time	Rate—WPM	Time	Rate—WPM
1:00	1782	5:30	324
1:10	1527	5:40	314
1:20	1337	5:50	305
1:30	1188	6:00	297
1:40	1069	6:10	289
1:50	972	6:20	281
2:00	891	6:30	274
2:10	822	6:40	267
2:20	764	6:50	261
2:30	713	7:00	255
2:40	668	7:10	249
2:50	629	7:20	243
3:00	594	7:30	238
3:10	563	7:40	232
3:20	535	7:50	227
3:30	509	8:00	223
3:40	486	8:10	218
3:50	465	8:20	214
4:00	446	8:30	210
4:10	428	8:40	206
4:20	411	8:50	202
4:30	396	9:00	198
4:40	382	9:10	194
4:50	369	9:20	191
5:00	356	9:30	188
5:10	345	9:40	184
5:20	334	9:50	181
		10:00	178

Lesson Nine
READING FLEXIBILITY AND TEST TAKING

In previous lessons you have been urged to employ an experimental attitude when approaching various portions of your speed reading activities. This was especially true when doing the Rate and Comprehension Test stories. To read fast you need to rid yourself of stereotyped rationalizations such as, "If I read fast I won't understand!"

To keep your mind "flexible" so you can continue to pursue speed reading goals, keep in mind these "experimental attitude" conditions as your practice and do the remaining activities presented in this book:

1) You must read down the page; I prefer simply to read down the page of words without using any "crutches" such as pacing down the page with a finger, hand, or other object. However, one of these three might work best for you and you should try them out.

2) Being overly concerned with comprehension can interfere with your learning a specific speed reading technique. The skill you are attempting to master is more important than worrying about comprehension. Once you can read fast, comprehension techniques (such as the preview) can be pursued.

3) Skim some practice-reading materials. Read some materials as fast as you can, reading all, or almost all, the words. Compare the two methods of speed reading again. Combine the two and make them a part of your speed reading style.

4) When reading stories for rate, you will have set a goal to read a certain number of WPM or to read the story within a certain amount of time. Review these two goal-setting methods in your mind. Which of the two produced the best results for you?

5) To provide yourself a base from which to project your reading rate to even higher levels, check your past reading rates using the records you have kept. Set your reading goals high, remembering that you will probably under-estimate your ability to read fast.

Some students quickly master speed reading skills and achieve high reading rates while other students take longer. There are a number of reasons for this discrepancy related to poor reading habits, rationalizations to overcome, and maybe to a degree, intelligence. The following is a true example of two speed reading students. Twins, a brother and sister, both very intelligent, began a speed reading course together. The girl rapidly progressed through the course attaining high reading rates with excellent comprehension. The boy experienced difficulty gaining a high reading rate as quickly as his sister. His comprehension was quite good but to gain a reading rate comparable to that of his sister he persevered four times as long in class. He finally reached a reading rate with which he was satisfied. Both these students have assured me over a period of years that they still have a high reading rate with excellent comprehension.

Speed readers who have gained high reading rates and who don't consciously make themselves read fast at all times tend to lose their high reading rates. A number of students who successfully completed a well-known speed reading course found their reading rate diminishing. They brushed up their speed reading techniques in a course that I offered and their former high reading rates rapidly returned.

Speed reading skills are somewhat universal. There are several ways to learn such skills. Using conventional speed reading techniques such as are presented in this book, using reading machines, or a combination of the two can result in speed reading success. No matter, you can learn to read fast regardless. A former student had achieved a very high reading rate in my course with quite satisfactory comprehension. She accompanied her father, whose company was paying the expense of taking a well-known speed reading course, to a preliminary reading rate screening test. The 15-year-old girl, who had had 35 hours of speed reading instruction, read *very fast* with 100% comprehension. She was accused of having taken the well-known course before.

OPENING STATEMENT

For each lesson you have kept records of your reading rate and comprehension. These scores show your progress but it is also interesting to compare your reading results with those scores that other students have achieved. Following are some general comments about these reading rates and you can compare your scores to help estimate your own progress in speed reading.

Past experience indicates that the students with low reading rates in the beginning of a speed reading course do not achieve the higher rates of those students who read quite fast in the beginning of the course. Naturally there are exceptions to this pattern. My advice is for students to rate their progress in a relative fashion. For example, if you read slowly in the beginning and doubled your rate (250 WPM to 500 WPM) — or read fast in the beginning and doubled your rate (500 WPM to 1000 WPM), relatively speaking, you have done equally well.

It has been determined that the human eye cannot see each printed word and read more than 800 WPM. It isn't necessary to read every word because skimming the printed material will provide the thoughts necessary for adequate comprehension. With concentration and effort I can read several thousand WPM. Mostly I read between 800 to 1200 WPM depending on the type of material being read and when and where I am reading. Remember that this is with satisfactory comprehension.

I've always had many students who read much faster than I read. Publishing reading rates that you could compare your own reading rates with has purposely been held to a minimum because such figures can provide somewhat false personal achievement goals. You have kept reading rate and comprehension records each week. You can see your progress in WPM. Have you doubled or tripled your reading rate from that which you attained at the beginning of the course? You know yourself! Are you reading faster? Do you feel that you have made the progress you had hoped for and expected by studying this book? All you have to do is check your Reading Rate Graph and measure your reading rate progress from the beginning until now. Other than as an "ego-massager" to yourself, or to tell friends about, the WPM you have achieved serves only as a guideline to what is truly most important — you are reading faster and comprehending well! This is the important thing that you have achieved.

SKILLS AND TECHNIQUES

This section is concerned with taking objective tests. It is primarily aimed at the student attending school who is faced, probably more often than that person would like, with having to take objective tests. All those people who have to take objective tests, including speed reading students taking their own comprehension tests at the end of each lesson, can apply the following general aspects of objective tests that are common to all:

1) Skim over the total test to gain an impression of its scope.

2) Your first impression of an answer to a question is most often correct. Unless you know you have chosen a wrong answer, go with your first impression.

3) No matter how many answer choices you have to the quesion being asked, you can usually narrow down the choices to two. Do this and then make your choice.

4) Often all answer choices will be partially correct. Choose the *most* correct answer.

5) Skip those questions that you don't know the answer to and go through the entire test answering those questions that you can before you come back to the unanswerable questions.

GOAL SETTING

Early in this book it was pointed out that learning to speed read employs a mechanical process. Mastery of such mechanical speed reading skills requires much repetition. With this in mind, let's review speed reading goals gleaned from all eight previous lessons:

1) Go to that place in your home or place of employment where you always, if possible, do your lessons.

2) Warm-up by reading some of the past Rate and Comprehension Test stories from Lessons One through Eight.

3) Allow yourself 30 seconds to preview the test story.

4) Understand what bad reading habits are and what you can do to overcome them. (See Lesson Three)

5) Always use the relaxed eye fix in the middle of the column or page of words and then read down!

6) Please review all those good reading practices that were presented in the Skills and Techniques section of Lesson Five.

7) Set a goal to read the Rate and Comprehension Test story in a certain number of WPM or within a certain amount of time. Refer to your past records to assist yourself in this goal.

8) As a way to preview a story, look for the five parts of a story: Setting, Characters, Action, Climax, and Conclusion.

9) Remember that the most natural speed reading style combines a) Reading all, or almost all, the words in the story and b) skimming.

10) Look for topic sentences in paragraphs when previewing and reading.

11) When learning to speed read don't be overly concerned with comprehension because it will interfere with the mastery of speed reading skills.

12) Maintain an open and experimental attitude as you take your Rate and Comprehension Tests.

13) Force yourself to read fast. The greatest reading rate gains tend to occur in the final lessons of the course. Refer to the Reading Rate Charts in Lesson One. Do you notice how the greatest WPM gains are toward he end of all the lessons?

14) Your most important goal shouldn't be always to compare your reading rate with normal or with someone else's reading rate, but just to read fast with comprehension.

15) Skim over objective tests before tackling each individual test item. Remember that the first impression you have of an answer to a question is most often correct. Narrow answer choices down to two and then choose. Choose the *most* correct answer. Skip questions you don't know the answers to and then come back to the unanswered questions.

* * * * * * * * * *

RATE AND COMPREHENSION TEST

Read the following story, "Monterey — 1842." Be sure to refer to the procedure for taking this test that was described under the Skills and Techniques section of Lesson One. Do this right now. *Do the following for this and for each of the ten Rate and Comprehension Tests in this book.*

1) Read the story,

2) Keep track of the time taken to read the story in minutes and seconds and *write it down,*

3) Take the comprehension test,

4) Use the chart at the end of the lesson to figure your reading rate (WPM),

5) Use the answer key at the end of the lesson to figure your comprehension level,

6) Chart your scores on the Reading Rate and Comprehension Graphs on pages 177 and 178.

7) You will need a watch, or some type of timepiece, on which to keep track of the time it takes you to read the test story,

8) Think of the speed reading goals presented in the Goal Setting Portion of this lesson before you begin to read the test story.

* * * * * * * * * *

* * Set your timepiece — read the story * *
MONTEREY — 1842

by Robert Haven

Today, with almost instant worldwide communication, statesmen and military leaders are on top of any incident practically from the moment it occurs and can react both immediately and appropriately. Before the development of transoceanic cables, radio, and the most recent satellite communication systems, there was, necessarily, a large time gap between the action and the reaction. The War of 1812, for example, would not have been declared at all had the leaders in Washington, D.C., been aware that most of the problems had already been resolved in London weeks before. Furthermore, the Battle of New Orleans, the United States' only real victory in that war, would not have been fought since the peace treaty ending the War of 1812 had been signed nearly a month earlier. Diplomats and military leaders far from their capitals were required to exercise a tremendous amount of judgment for they were obliged to operate in the dark. Their most recent news could be several months old by the time they received it. This was particularly true in the case of naval commanders like the Commodore Thomas ap Catesby Jones who, in 1842, commanded the U.S. Navy's Pacific Squadron.

In 1842 the relations between the United States and the Republic of Mexico were quite strained; indeed, war could have broken out at any moment. The primary cause of this tension was the Texas situation. Americans in Texas had successfully separated from Mexico, declared their independence, and applied to the United States for annexation. The southern part of the United States was enthusiastically in favor of this move, but many northerners opposed it as it would add more slave territory to the country. The Mexican government still considered Texas to be a part of Mexico and threatened war if their provinces were annexed. All through this period the expansionists and anti-expansionists jockeyed for position in the United States while Mexico watched warily.

Besides Texas, another Mexican region, California, was attracting the United States' attention. California was at this time only sparsely settled, consisting of a few small dusty villages that had grown up along the chain of missions begun in 1769. The principal economic activities were a rather sluggish trade in hides and tallow, and sea otter pelts. Most of these items were sold illegally to American traders since the Mexican government forbade any commerce with foreigners. Since there was no market in Mexico for their products the Californians paid little attention to the law and quite happily sold them to the Yankee traders. California was separated from the rest of Mexico by a vast expanse of desert or long sea voyage so the Mexican government's hold and control was very weak at best.

While the troubled young Republic of Mexico was unable or unwilling to pay much attention to California, the British and Russians, as well as the United States, had ideas of adding it to their empires. The most attractive feature of California at this time was San Francisco Bay, one of the finest natural harbors in the world. In 1835 President Andrew Jackson had offered Mexico $500,000 for it. California (with San Francisco) fit in very nicely with the Manifest Destiny of a United States spanning the continent. While Russia was indeed interested, the main rival for California was Great Britain, already well established in Canada and Oregon.

As tension mounted and the possibility of a war with Mexico became more likely, the threat of a British grab for California worried the United States State and Navy departments. It was believed that the British Navy would certainly move to seize California at the first outbreak of war. Then, as now, the United States Navy had plans for carrying on a war with any potential enemy or combination of enemies. In the event of a war with Mexico, the U.S. Pacific Squadron would immediately seize California to forestall a similar move by the British.

In 1842 Commodore Thomas ap Catesby Jones was appointed to command of the Pacific

Squadron. Jones, a veteran of nearly 37 years in the Navy, had fought pirates and smugglers in the Caribbean and the Gulf of Mexico, the British in the War of 1812, and in 1825 helped to foil a British attempt to take over the Hawaiian Islands. All in all, he had an excellent record as a naval officer. His orders on taking command were rather general: Simply sail about the Pacific until such time as he should receive new orders and all the while he was to keep an eye open for any British moves toward California.

While Jones and his flagship, *Cyane*, were in Callao (the port of Lima, Peru) a British squadron arrived. Jones regarded the British with mixed emotions. They were his chief rival in the Pacific, but it was good to have them where he could watch them. Also, they did speak the same language and, as was the custom in those days, the officers of the two nations exchanged visits. One night the British officers of the *Dublin* would dine aboard the *Cyane* and the next night the American officers would dine on the British ship. This had gone on for several days until one evening, while the officers of the *Dublin* were enjoying the *Cyane's* hospitality, a message arrived ordering them back to their ship at once. Thanking their American hosts but offering no explanation the British left. A short time later the *Dublin* weighed anchor and sailed out of Callao leaving Jones to ponder its abrupt and mysterious departure. Jones considered the few facts he had and concluded that somehow the British had received word that war had broken out between the United States and Mexico, and the *Dublin* had sailed to seize California. "Why else should they be secretive?" he reasoned. Immediately Jones called his men back to the ship and prepared to race the British to California.

Callao, Peru, is a long way from California, a voyage of many weeks in the sailing ships of that time, and all the way up Jones worried that the British with their head start would arrive at Monterey first. With every inch of canvas available the sailors of the *Cyane* extended themselves to overtake the *Dublin,* and lookouts anxiously scanned the horizon for any sign of the British.

On October 19, 1842, the *Cyane* arrived at Monterey, Alta California's capital. To Jones' great relief the Mexican flag was still flying over the Presidio and there wasn't a sign of the rival British ship. Immediately the gunners were called to their stations as Jones prepared to attack. A broadside was fired. The Mexicans in the Presidio signalled that they were unable to return the American salute as they had no powder. Jones replied that he was not saluting but attacking and demanded their immediate surrender!

The Mexican Governor, General Michaeltorrena, chose this moment to march his "Cholo Army" out to meet the enemy. They appeared to have been somewhat disoriented for they marched to Los Angeles, some four hundred miles to the south. The removal of the "Cholo Army," though it left Monterey defenseless, was a relief to the local residents for it would have taken an army twice the size to protect them from the depredations of the "Cholos."

Abandoned by the Governor and his army, and having no gunpowder, the remaining Mexican officials had no choice but to surrender to the American force. Jones was rowed ashore where he replaced the Mexican flag with the Stars and Stripes and proclaimed the annexation of California to the United States.

The next day, however, Jones' victory turned to ashes when he received information from someone recently arrived from Texas that the United States and Mexico were not at war. Jones immediately summoned the Mexican commandant and explained to him that he, Jones, had been mistaken. He apologized for his action, ran up the Mexican flag, and prepared to leave Monterey and California at once. The commandant declared that in view of the magnitude of the error he should first see Governor Michaeltorrena in Los Angeles. Somewhat reluctantly Jones agreed to this meeting.

The voyage from Monterey to San Pedro did not require the same speed as did the trip from Peru since Jones was by no means in any hurry to face the Mexican governor. Eventually the *Cyane* arrived in San Pedro where a company of Michaeltorrena's dragoons were waiting to escort him to the meeting in Los Angeles. An open carriage had been borrowed from one of the town's leading citizens for the occasion.

Los Angeles in 1842 was a far cry from the sprawling metropolis it is today. It was a collection of rather small adobe houses. Its streets were either dusty or muddy depending on the weather. On this occasion they were muddy due to a rainstorm that greatly discomfited the "Cholo Army" in its "advance" to Los Angeles.

When Jones' carriage arrived at the governor's temporary residence, Michaeltorrena came out to greet him. Jones immediately began to express his regrets for the incident at Monterey, but the governor interrupted him saying that they would discuss that later. First there was to be a state dinner party with all the leading lights of Los Angeles present.

All through the banquet Jones, seated next to the governor, attempted to bring up the business of Monterey but each time the governor put him off. At last the dinner was finished and Michaeltorrena rose to his feet to address the company and Commodore Jones. It was indeed a most serious act, an unprovoked attack on a friendly nation by the naval forces of the United States. It was, besides being a gross insult to the Republic of Mexico, the cause of great hardship and distress to the good people of Monterey to say nothing of the suffering endured by the troops of his army. The governor ended his speech by reading a list of demands to Jones that would in part compensate those who had suffered at Jones' hands. It was a long list and included a complete set of band instruments and uniforms to replace those ruined by the rain during his army's march to Los Angeles.

Commodore Jones responded to the effect that while he did indeed acknowledge his most serious error in judgment, he could not accede to the governor's demands for material compensation as he was not authorized to deliver U.S. Naval property to a foreign power. The Mexican governor's face was, for a moment, long with disappointment. Then he announced that there would be a dance across the street when the dinner party was adjourned.

Getting across the quagmire that was the street presented a considerable problem, but the resourceful governor solved it by providing a carriage drawn by a squad of soldiers in the traces. No further mention of the Monterey affair was made that night and towards morning, after a long night of merrymaking, the tired erstwhile Conqueror of California was returned to his ship at San Pedro.

While the meeting with Michaeltorrena had turned out to be quite pleasant, Jones was certain that when news of his misadventure reached Washington he could look forward to much rougher treatment. Indeed, the reaction in Washington was explosive and orders were sent out immediately relieving Jones of his command and summoning him back to Washington post haste. While Jones knew that such orders would certainly be sent, he also knew that it would be several months before they could reach him. In the meantime he would be sailing about the Pacific as directed by his original instructions, postponing the inevitable showdown with his superiors.

Several ships were dispatched to find Jones, but the Pacific is a very large ocean and they were unable to find him. For the better part of a year Jones eluded them. Finally, short of supplies, Jones returned to Washington to face the long delayed reckoning.

A new Congress, chosen in the November 1842 elections, was now in session and to Jones' good fortune it was dominated by expansionists. This Congress was generally inclined to admire the initiative of the Pacific Squadron's commodore. Indeed, some members were in favor of issuing Jones a commendation for his actions at Monterey.

The whole affair has elements of a comic opera, particularly when viewed from the vantage point of more than a century later, but the Mexican government was hardly amused for the United States' designs on California were clearly exposed.

The anti-expansionists, who opposed the addition of any more territory that might become slave states, were equally disturbed. The pro-expansionists, however, were in the driver's seat and although Jones did not receive a commendation for his "admirable initiative," and he was relieved of his command, in less than a year he was once more commanding the Navy's Pacific Squadron.

* * * * * * * * * *

IMMEDIATELY START TO ANSWER THE FOLLOWING TEN COMPREHENSION QUESTIONS. CIRCLE THE *MOST* CORRECT ANSWER. TAKE A REASONABLE AMOUNT OF TIME TO ANSWER THE QUESTIONS. YOU SHOULDN'T LOOK BACK INTO THE STORY FOR ANSWERS.

COMPREHENSION TEST NINE

___ 1) The War of 1812 and the Battle of New Orleans point out a) how unnecessary war can be, b) the importance of rapid communication, c) how important a role diplomacy can play.

___ 2) Which of the following countries seemingly was the chief adversary of the United States regarding possible aquisition of California from Mexico? a) Spain, b) Russia, c) Great Britain.

___ 3) Commodore Jones, of the United States Navy, apparently felt it was the appropriate time to seize California from Mexico as a result of a) word from Washington to do so, b) a British ship leaving a harbor in Peru. c) a declaration of war against Mexico

_____ 4) It appears that the chief reason for the surrender of Monterey to Commodore Jones was a) an error in judgment by the Mexican Army Commander, b) a weak defensive position of the fortress, c) the overwhelming superiority of the attacking United States fleet.

_____ 5) The day after the conquest of Monterey, Commodore Jones a) prepared to attack General Michaeltorrena in Los Angeles, b) returned control of Monterey to the Mexicans, c) proclaimed a state of war existed between the United States and Mexico.

_____ 6) When Commodore Jones appeared in Los Angeles, General Michaeltorrena a) greeted him in a rather regal fashion, b) engaged him in a decisive battle, c) had already returned to Monterey.

_____ 7) Jones realized that after his actions in California he would a) be greeted as a hero in Washington, b) be relieved of his command, c) be appointed as Governor of California.

_____ 8) A new United States Congress chosen in the 1842 elections was a) admiring of Commodore Jones' actions in California, b) inclined to declare war on Mexico immediately, c) for returning California to Mexican control.

_____ 9) Commodore Jones' actions at Monterey in 1842 probably played a major incident leading to a) Jones' execution for disobeying orders, b) friendship with Great Britain over the Oregon question, c) eventual war with Mexico.

___ 10) The main idea of this story seems to a) revolve around a series of comic opera mistakes, b) show the Mexicans of United States' intentions regarding California, c) show how important California was as an addition to the United States.

* * * * * * * * * *

CHECK YOUR ANSWERS AGAINST THE KEY ON PAGE 159. CONVERT YOUR READING TIME TO RATE USING THE CHART ON PAGE 159-160. REMEMBER, ONCE YOU HAVE CONVERTED READING TIME INTO WORDS PER MINUTE (WPM) IT IS NO LONGER NECESSARY TO KEEP A RECORD OF THE READING TIME THAT IT TAKES YOU TO READ EACH STORY. CHART YOUR READING RATE (WPM) AND COMPREHENSION SCORE ON THE READING RATE GRAPH AND READING COMPREHENSION GRAPH ON PAGES 177 AND 178.

* * * * * * * * * *

PRACTICE BEFORE THE NEXT LESSON

1) Turn back to some of the comprehension tests that you have taken in previous lessons. Apply the common aspects of all objective tests to those test questions, such as: Skimming the total test to gain an impression of its scope; remembering that first impressions of answers are most often correct; narrowing down answer choices to two and then choosing the most correct answer; and answering all questions you know the answers to, skipping those you aren't sure of before coming back to try and answer these questions. Can you see how these test skills apply to the taking of objective tests?

2) Choose a newspaper or story in your reading place and be "experimental" as your read down the page. Don't be overly concerned with

comprehension; force yourself to read fast, alternately skimming and then slowing down as necessary; choose a WPM or time goal after you have checked your past rates; and then set even higher rate goals.

3) Practice reading a variety of materials such as newspapers, magazines, stories, novels, charts, recipes, etc., to experience the full range of skills necessary for varying your reading rate according to the type and difficulty of the printed material being read.

* * * * * * * * * *

Answers — Comprehension Test Nine — 1) b, 2) c, 3) b, 4) a, 5) b, 6) a, 7) b, 8) a, 9) c, 10) a

* * * * * * * * * *

Time	Rate— WPM	Time	Rate— WPM
1:00	2131	3:50	556
1:10	1827	4:00	533
1:20	1579	4:10	511
1:30	1421	4:20	492
1:40	1279	4:30	474
1:50	1162	4:40	457
2:00	1065	4:50	441
2:10	984	5:00	426
2:20	913	5:10	412
2:30	852	5:20	400
2:40	799	5:30	387
2:50	752	5:40	376
3:00	710	5:50	365
3:10	673	6:00	355
3:20	639	6:10	346
3:30	609	6:20	336
3:40	581	6:30	328

Time	Rate—WPM	Time	Rate—WPM
6:40	320	10:00	213
6:50	312	10:10	210
7:00	304	10:20	206
7:10	297	10:30	203
7:20	291	10:40	200
7:30	284	10:50	197
7:40	278	11:00	194
7:50	272	11:10	191
8:00	266	11:20	188
8:10	261	11:30	185
8:20	256	11:40	183
8:30	251	11:50	180
8:40	246	12:00	178
8:50	241	12:10	175
9:00	237	12:20	173
9:10	232	12:30	170
9:20	228	12:40	168
9:30	224	12:50	166
9:40	220	13:00	164
9:50	217		

Lesson Ten
HOW TO KEEP YOUR
READING RATE HIGH

Don't limit yourself to a low reading rate! Almost to a person, at least initially, students underestimate their ability to read fast. A seemingly formidable barrier for speed reading students is reading 1000 WPM. Students I have known struggle with their rate to this point, plateau out, and then rationalize their inability to conquer this Mt. Everest. Could this be a corollary mental attitude such as the stock market reaching 1000 on the Dow Jones Industrial Average? So many students on the threshold of reading 1000 WPM finally break through and then progressively read faster and faster with little or no loss in comprehension.

You have learned to read fast. Probably in your lifetime you learned to ride a bicycle. Once you learned you never forgot. This is not true of speed reading as you will gradually lose your high reading rate unless you keep on using the speed reading techniques that you have mastered. There is no one "pearl of wisdom" that I can pass on to you that will forever guarantee you a high reading rate. Following are two suggestions that will help you to retain a high reading rate:

1) Be *very* conscious that you are trying to keep your reading rate high. This is a very important skill you will need to develop to maintain a high reading rate. I must constantly remind myself, when I find myself reading more slowly than I should to *speed it up!* Again, put the idea into your mind that you can and must read fast. I have heard hundreds of

testimonials that this simple idea is probably the single most important thing that you can do to help keep your reading rate high.

2) Be aware that you are performing the act of reading — not how you are reading or what you are reading — but that *you are reading!* Keep this idea tucked into a corner of your mind because it is most important to remind yourself that to read fast you must use those reading skills and techniques that you have learned and mastered.

OPENING STATEMENT

You may find yourself later on, in your speed reading pattern, seeing "blocks" of words as you read. You may have already noticed that when reading you don't just see a single line of words but can see several lines of words on one side of the page and then several lines of words on the other side of the page. As always you should be reading *down* the page. As your eye fixes perceive lines of words on the left of the page, and then on the right side of this page, as you move down the page of printed material, you make a kind of "S" movement with your eyes. After speed reading for a time I realized that I had developed this "S" pattern of reading without even being aware of it. Speed readers have mentioned that they too had developed this same general reading pattern so I feel that it must be a natural reading style when reading fast. So, master your speed reading techniques and if you find an "S" reading pattern developing, you have "arrived."

All readers tend to retain the basic fear that if they read fast they won't comprehend well. Throughout the entire book you have been encouraged to read fast and not be so concerned with comprehension. This was to enable you to gain the necessary skills to read fast and not be "hung-up" on comprehension which would hinder your mastery of speed reading techniques.

The following five sentences are very important when dealing wih comprehension as you read fast. After this lesson you will be on your own in reading in that you won't be operating within the confines of a speed reading lesson. As a result, your reading rate will probably *fall*. If your rate is very high, it will fall but will still remain at a high rate level! You should notice that *comprehension levels will rise* as a result of this *reduced reading rate!* So you see that you didn't really need to worry so much about comprehension after all.

SKILLS AND TECHNIQUES

By now you must be acutely aware that your reading style consists of both *skimming* and *reading more slowly*, at times, as your needs dictate. Whichever of the two skills that make up this combination that you are using to read fast depends on the material being read and your interest. Another way of looking at this combined reading style is whether the material being read is dull or interesting. Students have remarked that the more interesting something is that is being read the faster they read and conversely so if the material is dull reading. Yet, other students have said that just the opposite occurs when they read. Which is true of your reading style?

This is the final lesson in this book. You must look now to what has to be done to keep your rate high in the future. The following is a list of very important skills that you can pursue to do just that:

1) Keep on *skimming* as you read. Don't be afraid to do so because it just isn't necessary to read every word to comprehend well.

2) Always *preview* any materials where comprehension of what you have read is a must.

3) Remember the basic skills and techniques necessary to read with speed, such as using the relaxed eye fix in the middle of the column or page of words, reading down the page as fast as you can force yourself to, and looking for the topic sentences of paragraphs.

4) Be aware that you are *performing the act of reading* — not what or how you are reading — but that *you are reading!*

5) Constantly remind yourself that you need to use those speed reading skills to keep yourself reading fast and with comprehension. Use them or lose them!

GOAL SETTING

This is the final chance to read as fast as you can, using the materials in this book:

1) Warm-up on some stories in this book that you have already read. Use the relaxed eye fix; read down the column or page of words; pick out some topic sentences from the paragraphs; and force yourself to read just as fast as you can.

2) Establish a goal to read the Rate and Comprehension Test story the fastest that you have ever read. Set a goal in either words per minute (WPM) or time.

3) Remember that the greatest reading rate gains tend to occur in the final lessons of this speed reading course.

RATE AND COMPREHENSION TEST

Read the following story, "The Glaciers Are Coming — The Glaciers Are Coming!" Be sure to refer to the procedure for taking this test that was described under the Skills and Techniques section of Lesson One. Do this right now. *Do the following for this and each of the ten Rate and Comprehension Tests in this book.*

1) Read the story,

2) Keep track of the time taken to read the story in minutes and seconds and *write it down.*

3) Take the comprehension test,

4) Use the chart at the end of the lesson to figure your reading rate (WPM),

5) Use the answer key at the end of the lesson to figure your comprehension level,

6) Chart your scores on the Reading Rate and Comprehension Graphs on pages 177 and 178.

7) You will need a watch, or some type of timepiece, on which to keep track of the time it takes you to read the test story.

8) Think of the speed reading goals presented in the Goal Setting portion of this lesson before you begin to read the test story.

* * Set your timepiece — read the story * *

THE GLACIERS ARE COMING —
THE GLACIERS ARE COMING!
by Merrill L. Ream

World leaders, presently convened in Washington, D.C., have turned to a panel of eminent scientists in an effort to determine the approach rate of the advancing glaciers in the higher latitudes of the world. It appears that massive population shifts will be necessary to assist people in fleeing the rapidly approaching ice sheets.

The latest reports indicate that ice caps presently cover almost the northern one half of Canada and the Soviet Union. Scandinavia is almost completely covered by a sheet of ice. One half of Argentina is covered by ice and the tips of Africa and Australia have glaciers that are building in volume. Thousands of icebergs breaking off the Antarctic glaciers are floating in southern seas and have totally stopped ship navigation. Mountain ranges presently covered by ice sheets include the Himalayas and Pamirs in Asia, the Rocky Mountains in Canada and the United States, the Sierra Nevadas in the United States, the Andes in South America, and the Alps in Europe. Recent dispatches indicate that Montreal, Moscow, Stockholm, and Buenos Aires have been completely abandoned by their inhabitants to the encroaching ice masses.

The scientists relate that they fully expect the glaciers to eventually cover as much land as those did in the Pleistocene era. This means that roughly the northern one third of the United States, Europe, and Asia could be inundated by the swiftly advancing ice sheet. One third of South America and the southern parts of Africa and Australia could also be covered.

The new glacial age was spawned 50 years ago when the sudden shifting of the continental plates touched off calamitous volcanic eruptions worldwide. The resulting amount of volcanic dust remaining in the atmosphere has reduced solar radiation, which used to melt the glaciers, to such an extent that the average surface temperature of the world is eight degrees lower than before the eruptions. This decrease in temperature has allowed ice and snow to accumulate over land areas of the world to such proportions that glaciers have resulted.

Scientists say that the last ice age began almost one million years ago and ended about 10 to 15 thousand years ago. At present it appears that the only hope for people of the world is to retreat to habitable areas and hope that the volcanic dust obscuring the sun's radiation will filter out of the atmosphere more rapidly. This would allow increased heating of the earth's surface so as to melt the glaciers faster than they are capable of being formed.

Could the aforementioned events really take place? The story is based upon credible theories as to how ice sheets may have been formed in the past. Most of us know ice to be a crystalline and brittle substance that is encountered in only small amounts. However, where ice accumulates to a thickness of 300 feet or more the ice behaves as a semiliquid, plastic-like material that allows the ice sheet to spread out and move downhill.

Where conditions are favorable to allow snow to accumulate faster than it can melt, the surface melting, refreezing into ice, and the resulting compaction eventually turns into an icy mass which, with sufficient depth, becomes an active moving glacier. Glaciers that form in high mountains are characteristically long and narrow and occupy previously formed valleys. In polar regions the low temperatures allow ice to form into ice masses several thousand feet thick which spread and envelop surrounding landforms.

The upper thickness of a glacier is brittle and readily fractures into crevasses. The ice nearer the bottom is plastic and the glacier flows faster in the center. The rate diminishes toward the sides. The flowage rate of glaciers ranges from a few inches a day up to several feet a day for active glaciers. However, with a colder climate the flowage rate could accelerate.

Most glacial ice is heavily charged with rock fragments that carve a variety of landforms. Cirques are amphitheater-like formations in mountains where great amounts of snow and ice build up and from which glacial flows start down valleys. Horns are sharp peaks formed when three or more cirques intersect. A well known one is the Matterhorn in the Alps. If you cannot envision a horn, Disneyland in California has created a replica on which one can enjoy an exhilarating ride on a roller coaster type contrivance.

Glacial valleys are typically "U" shaped with other valleys intersecting the main valley from right angles usually high above the main valley floor. Once the glaciers are gone, streams plunge from the "hanging valleys," forming spectacular waterfalls, into the main "U" shaped valley. One of the best known examples of this is in the Yosemite National Park in California.

Glaciers carry huge amounts of rock debris. Like being on a conveyor belt, rocks are constantly deposited at the end of the glacier into formations called moraines. As glaciers advance and then recede, they leave their moraine signatures clearly on the landscape. The moraines are elevated above the surrounding land and in Europe roads have been built on top of them utilizing a naturally built roadbed. By and large the deposits of rock and gravel deposited by glaciers into moraines are not the best of materials to use for agricultural purposes.

Under-glacier streams formed at the bottom of the ice mass wend serpentine routes that leave characteristic streambeds known as eskers. Deep glacial grooves are carved on bedrock over which glaciers flow. The Great Lakes in the United States and Canada were carved and gouged from the landscape and the water melt from the retreating glaciers of the last ice age provided in the original water to fill them.

The Athabasca Glacier in Jasper National Park in the Canadian Rockies is a part of the Columbia Icefield. This well studied glacier has crevasses reaching depths of 150 feet. Beautiful blue sheens glow from the depths of the cracks in the ice due to light filtering down into the crevasses. Since 1841 the Athabasca Glacier has been steadily losing ice. Extremely high or low yearly snowfalls on the icefield reveal themselves in the movement some 20 years later.

Scientists feel that the retreat phase of glaciers could be near an end. Worldwide hot and cold climatic changes have occurred in the past. This cycle indicates that a cooler period is statistically possible which would produce an increased period of glacial activity.

A highlight of a trip to the Athabasca Glacier is a thrilling ride in a vehicle called a snowmobile. Entire busloads of tourists are loaded onto huge tracked vehicles and are taken out onto the ice of the glacier itself. A road winds to the leading edge of the glacier and viewers can walk up to the rock moraines deposited by the glacier in the past and again view the beautiful blue colors radiating from fractures in the ice. Tourists are cautioned against stepping into quick sand-like pools of liquefied sand called "glacial glop." This writer saw a man sink to his hips in "glop" before he could be pulled out.

Glaciers actually grind rock to the consistency of flour and this pulverized rock is termed glacial flour. In the summer as the glaciers beat a melting retreat, the glacial flour ground during the winter washes into streams and lakes and is suspended there, giving the water a milky quality. Colors range from gray to turquoise. Peyto Lake in the Canadian Rockies, during the summer melt, assumes a turquoise color from the glacial flour and truly provides a magnificent sight to view. As winter approaches, freezing temperatures halt the flow of glacial flour and Peyto Lake, like countless other glacial lakes, assumes a deep blue color.

It doesn't appear that the world will have to contend with a new ice age in the near visible future. Presently remnants of the ice age are still with us and it is something to enjoy rather than be feared. Spectacular glacial scenery is enjoyed in the Alpine Mountains of Europe. Glacier National Park, located in Montana, contains most of these unique features found only in an "ice age" setting. Lake Louise in the Canadian Rockies combines a marriage of glaciers, mountains, and a lake into one of the most impressive settings on earth.

* * * * * * * * * *

IMMEDIATELY START TO ANSWER THE FOLLOWING TEN COMPREHENSION QUESTIONS. CIRCLE THE *MOST* CORRECT ANSWER. TAKE A REASONABLE AMOUNT OF TIME TO ANSWER THE QUESTIONS. YOU SHOULDN'T LOOK BACK INTO THE STORY FOR ANSWERS.

* * * * * * * * * *

COMPREHENSION TEST TEN

___ 1) Which of the following is not a place where glaciers are likely to form? a) oceans, b) high mountains, c) polar regions.

___ 2) It was pointed out that ice sheet during the Pleistocene era covered about a) the land area of all the continents, b) one third of the United States, Europe, and Asia, c) one half of the oceans of the world.

___ 3) The story indicates that the one thing that set off massive volcanic eruptions was a) a lowering of the earth's temperature, b) a movement of the earth's magnetic field, c) a shifting of the continental plates.

___ 4) The reader can assume that the events described in the beginning of this story could a) actually have occurred, b) occur in the future, c) not happen too often.

___ 5) Basically glaciers are formed when a) the temperature becomes quite cold, b) large bodies of water begin to freeze over, c) ice and snow accumulate faster than they can melt.

___ 6) The lower portion of glaciers, with sufficient thickness, becomes a) brittle and crystalline, b) plastic, c) slippery.

___ 7) One of the best known peaks in the world that has been formed by glaciers is a) Mt. McKinley, b) a cirque, c) the Matterhorn.

___ 8) "U" shaped valleys are typically formed by glaciers in a) mountainous regions, b) polar regions, c) continental regions.

___ 9) A study of the Athabasca Glacier in the Canadian Rockies generally shows that a) glaciers can move at a rapid rate, b) people can safely travel on a glacier, c) the glacier is receding.

___ 10) Mainly this story is about a) the possibility that a new ice age could occur with changes in the climatic cycle, b) those unique features that glaciers possess, c) how glaciers affect the landscape.

* * * * * * * * * *

CHECK YOUR ANSWERS AGAINST THE KEY ON PAGE 176. CONVERT YOUR READING TIME TO RATE USING THE CHART ON PAGE 176. REMEMBER, ONCE YOU HAVE CONVERTED READING TIME INTO WORDS PER MINUTE (WPM) IT IS NO LONGER NECESSARY TO KEEP A RECORD OF THE READING TIME THAT IT TAKES YOU TO READ EACH STORY. CHART YOUR READING RATE (WPM) AND COMPREHENSION SCORE ON THE READING RATE GRAPH AND READING COMPREHENSION GRAPH ON PAGES 177 AND 178.

* * * * * * * * * *

PRACTICE FROM NOW ON

The ideas presented in this section are so very important to help you to keep on reading fast because there are no more lessons. You are now on your own! All of this book's speed reading activities in which you have been engaged were designed to help you establish a base from which to maintain high, and actually to move on to higher, reading rates. All this can occur, of course, with satisfactory comprehension.

From this point what is necessary to maintain your high speed reading rate? Suppose you are still not satisfied with your present reading rate — what can you do?

1) Any practice-type activities that you do from now on should simply consist of speed reading all materials that you read.

2) Remember that you can always review any of the past lessons presented in this book to reinforce speed reading skills and techniques.

3) Remind yourself that you are capable of reading faster than you generally believe.

4) Be so very aware that you are performing the act of reading — not how or what you are reading — but that you are reading! This will help you to recall and use those skills and techniques which you have mastered and are necessary to keep your reading rate high.

5) Earlier in this lesson it was pointed that you might find yourself reading "blocks of words" on either side of the page as you read down the page, making a sort of "S" pattern. This seems to be a natural way to read fast and your reading style might eventually manifest itself in this type of pattern.

6) Chances are that your reading rate might fall when you are removed from the reading lesson situation presented in this book. From now on there will be no new skills to master, no more tests to take, and no more clock to time your reading rate. So, removed from the confines of this situation, don't be alarmed if your reading rate tends to fall a bit. This is a very natural thing that can happen.

7) Your comprehension level tends to rise as your reading rate falls. I have had countless testimonials from former students attesting to this fact. Also research evidence shows this to be generally true. However, your reading rate should still remain at a very high level. You will eventually strike a balance between a high reading rate and satisfactory comprehension that will be appropriate for you.

8) You must force yourself to read fast because you will tend to regress to lower reading rates and possibly reacquire those bad reading habits that made you read slowly in the first place.

9) If you have gained only one speed reading skill through mastery of the materials in this book, the skill that would contribute most to a higher reading rate and comprehension level is the use of the preview. The preview helps you to know a little about what you are going to read and consequently you can read with greater speed and comprehension.

10) Your reading style probably consists of both skimming and reading more slowly at times. This is a natural way of reading fast and you should use it whenever and for whatever you read.

11) To help check your reading rate in the future, divide the number of words in the story by the amount of time taken to read the story to get your WPM. To review this process refer to the Skills and Techniques section of Lesson Eight.

12) Throughout this entire book you have been exposed to reading materials gauged to be on an average level. This was purposely done because to master the skills and techniques of speed reading requires practice using simpler reading materials. Now that you have gained the skills necessary read fast, apply them to everything that you read from now on. Adjust your reading rate as necessary according to the type of materials being read.

13) To further increase your reading rate, keep on using those same skills and techniques that you have already mastered. They will help you move on to even higher reading rates. The reading rate that

you now possess is not the ultimate. With concentration and practice, using the speed reading skills that you now possess, you can read at higher reading rates.

* * * * * * * * *

Answers — Comprehension Test Ten — 1) a, 2) b, 3) c, 4) a, 5) c, 6) b, 7) c, 8) a, 9) c, 10) b

* * * * * * * * * *

Time	Rate—WPM	Time	Rate—WPM	Time	Rate—WPM
1:00	1374	3:50	358	6:40	206
1:10	1178	4:00	344	6:50	201
1:20	1031	4:10	328	7:00	196
1:30	916	4:20	317	7:10	192
1:40	824	4:30	305	7:20	187
1:50	749	4:40	294	7:30	183
2:00	687	4:50	284	7:40	179
2:10	634	5:00	275	7:50	175
2:20	589	5:10	266	8:00	172
2:30	550	5:20	258	8:10	168
2:40	515	5:30	250	8:20	165
2:50	485	5:40	244	8:30	162
3:00	458	5:50	236	8:40	159
3:10	434	6:00	229	8:50	156
3:20	412	6:10	223	9:00	153
3:30	393	6:20	217	9:10	150
3:40	375	6:30	211		

Reading Rate Record Graph

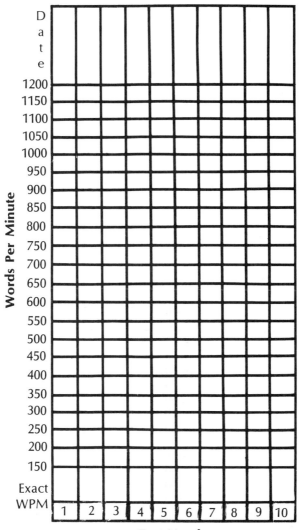

Test Number

Reading Comprehension Record Graph

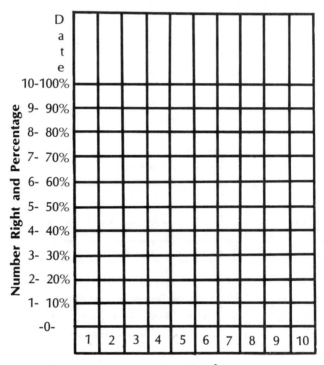

Test Number

Other Popular Books from Sheed Andrews and McMeel:

*The First Practical Pyramid Book: Free Energy for Beauty, Health,
    Gardening, Food Dehydration, and Meditation*
By Norman Stark $12.00 (cloth); $5.95 (paper)
The Formula Book
By Norman Stark $10.00 (cloth); $5.95 (paper)
The Formula Book 2
By Norman Stark $10.00 (cloth); $5.95 (paper)
The Formula Book 1 and 2 Slipcased Gift Pack
By Norman Stark $11.90 (paper)
Oven Drying: The Best Way to Preserve Foods
By Irene Crowe $5.95
Good Earth Almanac A to Z Dictionary of Health Food Terms
By Michael Balfour and Judy Allen $2.95 (paper)
Good Earth Almanac Old Time Recipes
By Mark Gregory $1.95 (paper)
Good Earth Almanac Natural Gardening Handbook
By Mark Gregory $1.95 (paper)
Good Earth Almanac Survival Handbook
By Mark Gregory $1.95 (paper)
All the Things Your Mother Never Taught You
By Charlotte Slater $4.95 (paper)
Things Your Mother Never Taught You About Car Care and Repair
By Charlotte Slater $2.50 (paper)

If you are unable to obtain these books from your local bookseller,
they may be ordered from the publisher. Enclose payment
with your order.

Sheed Andrews and McMeel, Inc.
6700 Squibb Road
Mission, Kansas 66202